The Complete Shadow Work Workbook & Journal

The Complete SHADOW WORK Workbook & Journal

Exercises and Prompts
to Prioritize Your Well-Being
and Heal Old Wounds

KELLY BRAMBLETT

callisto
publishing
an imprint of Sourcebooks

Copyright © 2024 by Callisto Publishing LLC
Cover and internal design © 2024 by Callisto Publishing LLC
Illustrations by Shutterstock: © Bibadash (frame); © Kozyrina Olga (floral pattern)
iStock/Getty Images: © Natouche (eye); © MaryliaDesign (leaf); © Tetiana Lazunova (mirror)
Art Director: Regina Stadnik
Art Producer: Samantha Ulban
Editor: Brian Sweeting
Production Editor: Jael Fogle
Production Manager: Holly Haydash

Callisto Publishing and the colophon are registered trademarks of Callisto Publishing LLC

Published by Callisto Publishing LLC C/O Sourcebooks LLC
P.O. Box 4410, Naperville, Illinois 60567-4410
(630) 961-3900
callistopublishing.com

Printed and bound in the United States of America.
VP 10 9 8 7 6 5 4 3 2 1

I dedicate this book to all those
who are doing their work, healing
their wounds, and continuously
striving toward self-improvement.
Thank you for doing your part.

CONTENTS

INTRODUCTION

Welcome to this new and exciting journey. My name is Kelly Bramblett, and I will be guiding you through the shadow work laid out for you in this workbook. I am a trauma care specialist, emotional freedom technique (EFT) practitioner, life coach, law of attraction practitioner, and Usui Reiki Master teacher. Beyond all the certifications and titles, though, I am a survivor of trauma and someone who is deeply motivated to help heal the collective by teaching others how to first heal themselves.

The most valuable lessons I learned weren't obtained through classes. They were given to me through my personal shadow work journey back to health, which spanned more than twenty years. I moved at a pace of two steps forward, one step back. This slow forward movement occurred primarily because I did not possess the tools I needed to process and heal my wounded self. The learning was slow, but the lessons were potent. Over time, as my life improved, I knew I wanted to teach others all that I had learned so that they didn't have to spend twenty years figuring it out like I did. What you learn in this workbook will support you for the rest of your life if you apply the practices and techniques consistently.

Even though my shadow work journey was based around healing my unresolved wounding, there are many layers to this work. The shadow is just another word for the unconscious mind. A lot happens beneath the surface of our awareness. Our limiting beliefs, conditioned thinking, unresolved wounding, shame, ego self, and deepest fears are all aspects of the shadow mind. These things combined are the cause of our toxic cycles, triggering, and general dissatisfaction.

This workbook is for anyone who feels stuck or has a longing for more. It is for those of you who have a true desire to understand yourself and are willing to look at the uncomfortable aspects of your hidden psyche with the energy of love, compassion, and radical self-acceptance. I know this may sound a little (or maybe even very) scary right now, but I will be here to gently guide you the entire way by providing you with evidence-based tools that will continue to support you long after you finish working through this book.

While this workbook has been created to empower you so that you feel confident doing this work on your own, it is not a replacement for professional treatment such as therapy. If at any time you do feel that this work is triggering emotions or intrusive thoughts that feel too heavy to manage alone, seek help. There is no shame in admitting when we need support. None of us are meant to go it alone through this life.

It's true that shadow work can be quite uncomfortable, but it is also rewarding and enjoyable. Remember, we never stop growing or learning. Allow this truth to bring you into relaxation as you work through this book. Take a deep breath, and when you are ready, let's get started!

How to Use This Book

This book is divided into two parts. Part 1 is an introduction to help you gain a deeper understanding of what shadow work is and how it can benefit your life.

Part 2 is a workbook with six chapters featuring interactive exercises, suggested practices you can implement into your daily routine, and a handful of case studies sprinkled in along the way. Each of these chapters also includes a separate journaling section with guided writing prompts, designed to help you reflect on your thoughts, feelings, and accomplishments as you progress on your shadow work journey.

How you choose to use this book is entirely up to what feels best for you. You can work through from beginning to end, or you can explore different topics and allow your intuition to guide you to what is most needed at that time. Whichever method you choose, just remember it's all about the journey, not the destination. There is much wisdom in this age-old saying when it comes to doing inner work and personal development. Take your time and allow each lesson to be integrated fully to aid you in creating a healthy shift in your life. These practices should not be rushed through or treated as if you are simply checking tasks off a to-do list. Rather, these lessons and concepts should be applied consistently to successfully create new habits. Sustainable change and growth happen one subtle step in the right direction at a time. There is no need to rush.

PART I

An Introduction to Shadow Work

The first part of this book will be your foundation, creating stability through a complete understanding of what shadow work is and what it is not. I will take you on a deep dive into the exploration of the shadow self, calling attention to how our limiting beliefs and conditioned way of thinking are created. Understand that we all have a shadow side, and while your first instinct may be to feel ashamed or embarrassed by what you discover along the way, with the right mindset, what you learn about these clouded aspects of yourself will serve as some of your greatest tools for growth. In time, you will even learn to feel gratitude for the painful lessons, inflicted wounding, and uncomfortable energies stored in the unconscious mind. However, first you need awareness and understanding of how your shadow self has been molded from your past experiences. This clarity ensures that you can work through the processes with ease and self-assuredness, which sets you up for success and sustainability in your growth.

CHAPTER 1

MEETING YOUR SHADOW SELF

This chapter is heavily focused on the explanation of what makes up our shadow aspects and how they develop throughout our lives. There are many different facets that are involved in the never-ending development of the shadow self. The idea isn't to snuff out or do away with these parts that make up the whole of who you are. Rather, the goal is to learn how to love, appreciate, observe without judgment, and integrate your shadow without identifying with it. In doing so, you create space between reaction and response, which allows you to make healthy choices no matter what you are faced with.

You will learn how to soothe your inner child, dismiss your inner critic, and quiet the ego, which will allow you to operate from a space of clarity. Mindset is also paramount to this work and will be addressed in this chapter. You will learn about the chaos that is often created when we try to ignore, run from, or suppress the shadow. In addition, I will highlight in detail the many ways in which shadow work will benefit you in all areas of your life.

ADDRESSING CONDITIONED THINKING

I remember fondly a client with whom I worked early in my coaching career named Sara. She came to me because she felt she had an unhealthy relationship with food, which she described as a food addiction. Her concerns were more about the quality of the food she was consuming as opposed to the quantity.

As we started unpacking her history with trauma, she shared with me how she had been the scapegoat child in a large family. Her verbally and physically abusive mother instilled fear in and controlled all members of the family, including her docile father, who was never abusive himself but also never intervened on her behalf. She shared with me one day that her mother used to regularly beat her with her shoe while screaming, "You are a failure!" over and over again.

When I started working with Sara, she aspired to be a coach and a writer, but this limiting belief that was created in early childhood had convinced her that she wasn't good enough to do this work. Her dissatisfaction in her current job and life led her to rely on food for comfort to fill the void created from her painful past. I worked with her to confront these limiting beliefs and guided her through practices that helped her release years of stored emotions in the body and shift her thinking. The last time we spoke, she had two pro bono clients and was busy working on her general life-coaching certification.

WHAT IS THE SHADOW SELF?

The term *shadow self* was coined by Carl Jung, the popular Swiss psychoanalyst, though you may not know this work is based on any kind of science from the woo-woo explanations that are floating around the internet these days. There is really nothing mystical about the shadow self, even though there is something very mysterious about what remains hidden and buried. These aspects are often the parts of us that we feel ashamed or embarrassed of, which is one reason we may avoid acknowledging them.

I frequently ask my clients who are resisting this work if they feel they are perfect. One hundred percent of the time and without hesitation they will answer, "Of course not!" My next question is always "Then why do you feel so ashamed about being an imperfect being, just like every other person on the planet?" This seems to help them lean into a less judgmental and more accepting space of self-observation. Perfection is not the goal, nor is it a part of the human experience. The objective should always be awareness and consistent growth. We all have a shadow with which to contend, so there is no need to feel as if yours makes you less than anyone else or unworthy of accomplishing your life goals.

HOW DOES THE SHADOW SELF DEVELOP?

The shadow self is simply a part of the human condition, which means we already have the capacity for hosting the attributes of the shadow from the moment we take our very first breath. It is hardwired in the most primitive parts of the brain, passed down to modern-day humans from our ancient ancestors who needed the ego and the fight-or-flight activation to ensure the survival of our species. Now these parts of our psyche serve a very different purpose: helping us develop a deeper level of emotional maturity.

We are impacted by our unique experiences throughout the entirety of our lives. The brain is constantly receiving information from our outer stimuli. If we are identified with the ego, this information will be filtered through that lens, and we may act in ways that aren't in alignment with our higher consciousness. Have you ever lost your temper, said things you didn't mean to someone you loved, and felt guilty later, once you had returned to a more stable state of mind? This happens when we act outside of our core integral belief system, which can easily occur when we lack awareness of our shadow selves.

Childhood and Family Life

Many of the conditioned thinking and unhealthy belief systems we hold in the unconscious mind are created in childhood and continue to evolve, becoming more damaging to our lives as we get older. This is why a big part of shadow work involves the exploration of our earliest memories and our childhood environments. The trust that a child instinctively feels toward their parental figures will lead them to accept whatever they are told and shown without question. For example, a parent who withholds affection and praise can create abandonment wounds for the child. As a defense mechanism, the child matures into an adult who remains emotionally unavailable. As a result, they have difficulty maintaining healthy relationships, and a cycle is created.

Traumatic Experiences and Memories

Our unresolved traumatic experiences take up a lot of room in the shadow aspects of the psyche, especially those from early life, when our brains were still developing foundational ideas of the world. Trauma left undealt with can lead to spiraling into the depths of destructive living. Working in trauma care, I see a lot of people who struggle to maintain a healthy mindset, often battling issues like addiction, low self-esteem, people-pleasing, and an inability to understand and create healthy boundaries. When you follow the breadcrumbs, almost all toxic behavior and patterns can be traced back to wounding that has festered.

Perceived Shameful Experiences

Shame plays a major role in the human saga, but it should not be confused with its energetic cousin, guilt. Healthy guilt serves an important role, alerting us to when we have acted outside of our set moral standards, and allows us the opportunity to realign with our core values and integral belief system. Guilt turns into shame when we can't forgive ourselves or when we feel helpless to control the action that is causing us to feel guilty. An individual who has experienced ongoing traumatic events will often develop unhealthy guilt and shame, feeling responsible for the behaviors and actions of others. The energy of shame gets stored away in the unconscious mind, affecting how we feel about ourselves, how we allow others to treat us, and how worthy we feel of living a good life.

Why a Receptive Mind Is Crucial

A healthy mindset and a well-regulated nervous system are fundamental to doing this work. You want to be open-minded enough to be able to step outside of your comfort zone but sufficiently regulated to do so in a centered and grounded way. Before starting any shadow work practice, I always suggest taking a few moments for awareness and intentionality. Practice slowing and lengthening the breath, inhaling through the nose and exhaling through the nose. Scan the body and take note of any places where you are holding on to tension or clenching your muscles. Allow yourself to release tension with the exhalation, feeling yourself relax. You may even choose to set the intention of remaining loving, compassionate, and nonjudgmental toward yourself.

If at any time while working through this book you begin to feel overwhelmed, anxious, or too triggered—all signals of a dysregulated nervous system—pause to practice this breathwork technique. Paying attention to the subtle shifts in your body will support you in all aspects of your life. If you want to make this practice even more dynamic, add it to your daily routine. You can challenge yourself by extending the time you spend in this space each day. Don't be discouraged if at first you can hold this awareness for only a few minutes at a time; this will improve with consistency. Your breath is one of your greatest tools, so use it as needed to drop back into the body, ground down, and return to your center.

THE DANGERS OF SUPPRESSING YOUR SHADOW

It did not take long for me to become aware of an obvious connection between my clients who had stored trauma in the body and things like autoimmune disorders, fibromyalgia, and other types of physical disease—or dis-ease. When we repress aspects of the shadow in an attempt to bypass the discomfort, the discomfort will take some other form. While avoidance may provide a quick fix, hiding away what we deem to be unpleasant or uncomfortable *will* take a toll. Not only will suppression have a negative effect on the physical body, but it also can result in far more intense emotional symptoms as well, showing up as anxiety, depression, and discontentment.

According to the Centers for Disease Control and Prevention's Heart Disease Facts, one person dies every thirty-six seconds in the country from cardiovascular disease, making this "the leading cause of death for men, women, and people of most racial and ethnic groups in the United States." Hundreds of studies link stress, anxiety, and various mental disorders to heart attack and heart disease. The message is clear: To live our healthiest, we must learn processing and coping skills to navigate life's ups and downs. Not only does shadow work help you process things from the past, but it also facilitates a growth mindset and promotes healthy awareness in the present moment. This allows you to handle challenges that arise in a way that prevents them from being stored in the subconscious mind, ultimately leading to a deeper level of health.

Keep Track of Your Journey

One thing I was taught in my emotional freedom technique (EFT) certification training was to always have the client rate, on a scale of one to ten, how they were feeling prior to the session and then again after the session was complete. The reason for this is that the mind tends to forget where we started out once we move into a better space, and so it can be difficult to gauge improvement. Practitioners have found that when they don't implement this evaluation, clients tend to report little improvement because they forget their emotional frame of reference along the way. As evaluation became a common part of the practice of EFT, results improved because clients had a way to compare how they felt before and after treatment.

Likewise, keeping a record of your own journey through journaling or note-taking will provide you with the same kind of points of reference for comparison. Taking time to occasionally reflect on what you have recorded will often lead to even more revelations in hindsight. This practice will also help you better identify your wins, which will keep you motivated and moving forward along your journey. You may choose to write down your goals, manifestations, or intentions while also recording the ups and downs of your shadow work journey as you feel intuitively called. This will also be beneficial if you are working with a therapist.

THE BENEFITS OF ACKNOWLEDGING YOUR SHADOW

While the thought of doing this work may feel burdensome, I assure you the benefits make it well worth the time and effort. I have said this time and time again in my work: We are meant only to visit our shadows, not to dwell there for eternity. Your adventures into the darkness make the time spent in your light much more fulfilling. Integration happens when you create positive new habits. That realization makes the work feel a lot less intimidating and a lot more rewarding. It becomes second nature, requiring less effort on your part. Relationships improve, self-love grows strong, and increased confidence opens the doors to greater opportunities and success. The subtle progression of growth through personal development practices will create a massive shift over time, improving every area of your life.

Prioritize Your Well-Being and Healing

I know we all have full schedules and are juggling a multitude of responsibilities, but the number one priority must be our own health and well-being. Meeting our needs guarantees that we can show up for those responsibilities with as many internal resources as possible. When we continuously take time to fill our own cup and confront the tough issues showing up with ease and grace, we bring our best selves to all parts of our lives. In addition, we set a positive example for others by prioritizing our needs and normalizing self-care and holistic health practices that have been largely stigmatized in modern-day society, where being busy is glorified and seen as a false sign of success.

Break Free of Destructive Patterns

Shadow work is about bringing what is in the dark into the light—or, in other words, bringing awareness to the subconscious. As you do this, you will naturally begin to become aware of toxic cycles and destructive patterns in your life. Awareness is the first step. Once that piece is in place, you can create an actionable plan to release harmful habits. You can do this by intentionally adopting healthier habits. Anytime we clear away toxic patterns of behavior, we make space, which we can then fill intentionally, so the unconscious mind does not run the show. This is how we can break free of the invisible chains that bind us to harmful habits and cycles.

Heal Old Wounds and Release What Doesn't Serve You

Everyone experiences trauma somehow; that is life. Acknowledging and releasing trauma is a fundamental aspect of personal development. When we choose to address the wounding of our past with love, compassion, acceptance, and forgiveness, we allow ourselves to live more satisfying and enjoyable lives. The good news is that your suffering is not in vain. Your past painful experiences serve a higher purpose—allowing you the opportunity to rediscover the true expression of your soul through healing. When viewed from this mindset, pain becomes a powerful tool, offering valuable lessons that bring you into a deeper awareness of yourself.

Improve Every Part of Your Life

Curating a consistent routine that involves personal development offers limitless opportunities for improvement. Learning how to be responsive as opposed to reactive puts you in the driver's seat of your experiences. Life stops feeling like it's happening to you, and you begin to recognize the dance between intentionality and accountability in connection to how satisfied you feel. Your relationships improve as you cultivate a healthy perspective that centers around nonjudgmental observation. You will develop a healthy love of self through your dedication to improvement and will find ease in establishing and holding appropriate boundaries. Life becomes steeped in richness and meaning, opening you up to a deeper, more fulfilling and purposeful way of experiencing the world.

Feel Empowered to Be Who You Are, Flaws and All

There is nothing more empowering than showing up to the world authentically—unapologetically as you truly are, comfortably and without concern for what others might think. Radical self-acceptance is about loving all your parts, being gentle with yourself when you stumble, and knowing that your flaws—brought into being through your humanity—do not make you unworthy of receiving. Total freedom is birthed from inner validation, unbinding you from the need to be liked, removing fear of others' opinions and judgments. When you know yourself inside and out, no one can convince you of anything different, and that is a powerful place to be. You become unshakable.

Key Takeaways

As you learned in this chapter, your shadow is developed through many different experiences throughout your lifetime. Yet the benefits of understanding how this part of you affects your life in ways big and small are infinite. Let's recap what was covered:

- There is nothing mystical about the shadow self, despite some of the misinformation floating around the internet. Your shadow self is simply a combination of your past wounding, limiting beliefs, deepest fears, conditioned thinking, and perceived shameful experiences contained within the unconscious mind.

- The shadow self is impacted by and developed from several key components, including your early childhood experiences and family dynamics, past traumatic experiences, and perceived shameful behavior. Your inner narrative and limiting beliefs are influenced by how you process the information contained within these parts of your life experience.

- Avoidance or suppression of the shadow has negative impacts on health, including the physical body, emotional body, and mental body, as these are all connected to one another and tied to the subconscious mind.

- Shadow work will help you deepen your understanding of yourself in a safe, loving, and compassionate way. It leads to healing and allows improvement and growth to happen in all areas of your life.

CHAPTER 2

Understanding Shadow Work

In this chapter, we will continue to explore the shadow and how shadow work can help you confront challenges in a more balanced and grounded way. We will investigate the never-ending exploration of the self and the many ways this work can benefit your life long after it's done. We'll also cover how to cultivate a healthy relationship with your shadow. You will learn how to transform your mindset to one that will fully support your journey, bringing an energy of ease to your life.

Here, you'll find an in-depth explanation of the purpose, development, and importance of the shadow, clearing the way for you to embrace this aspect of yourself with loving-kindness. It is my deepest hope that, armed with the knowledge to move forward from a place of empowered understanding, you feel fully prepared, confident, and inspired to embark on the practices and exercises ahead.

The Four Pillars of Shadow Work in Action

Over the years, through the process of writing, teaching, and mentoring, I developed what I often refer to as the four pillars of healing all unresolved wounding. These four pillars are the essence of all shadow work and have been the foundation of my work as a trauma support and mindset coach (i.e., a shadow work coach). The four pillars are (1) nervous system self-regulation, (2) mindset, (3) radical self-love and acceptance, and (4) forgiveness of yourself and others. I have had the honor of witnessing firsthand how working through these concepts can transform lives.

Take Autumn, for example, a woman who came to me because she was unable to relax. She lived in constant fear of not having enough time in her life, which caused her to feel as if she were always behind. Because she also struggled with low self-esteem, she expressed to me that she felt like a failure. She feared her husband might leave her and was mentally and emotionally taxed. She enrolled in my eight-week one-on-one program, during which we tackled each pillar, incorporating inner child work, addressing her past trauma, and forging a new mindset. I also offered her tools that helped her regain her confidence. During our time working together, she started prioritizing her need for guilt-free rest and was able to gain a healthy perspective on time that allowed her to actually accomplish more, strategizing from her newfound clarity.

INVESTIGATE YOUR SHADOW SELF THROUGH SHADOW WORK

Human beings have been intrigued by the unseen, unknown, and hidden aspects of our psyche for as long as we have been recording life. The way in which we view inner work has evolved as our understanding of the human brain and psychology has grown. Groundbreaking epigenetic studies are proving that our thoughts and feelings impact us on a cellular level by affecting the way that our DNA expresses itself, such as by activating or deactivating certain genes. Shadow work quite literally changes us on a cellular level.

As science finally starts to catch up with what spiritual teachers have been sharing for thousands of years, ancient tools and techniques are being rediscovered. Practices like mindfulness and meditation help regulate the nervous system, which sets the foundation for all other work to be done. Intentional movement like dance and yoga help create the body-mind connection, which is the remedy for dissociation, a common trauma response. Self-care and forgiveness bring us to a more nurturing and compassionate place, helping us live more joyful lives and facilitating healthy relationships and a sense of community. There really is nothing new under the sun when it comes to shadow work, but thankfully, we now have evidence-based tools bringing more validity to this work.

THE PROCESS OF SHADOW WORK LEADS TO PERSONAL GROWTH

The beautiful thing about this work is that it isn't reserved for some. It is available to anyone who is willing to dig deep and look inward with curiosity and acceptance. With just a little guidance, you can safely work within the shadow to effectively heal, grow, and transform yourself and your life.

It is common for there to be discomfort and triggering along the way. You may even find that engaging in shadow work stirs up painful emotions and memories. You may be called to explore past experiences that you would rather forget about completely. Don't worry; you'll gain the tools to cope with any discomfort that may arise. There is no need to fear the processes. You will soon find that when you take steps to integrate your shadow as opposed to repressing it, the work not only becomes rewarding but comes with new ease. The suggested practices, exercises, and journal prompts provided in the second part of this book are all meant to help you explore the shadow freely and deeply.

Welcome Your Shadow with Honesty and Vulnerability

One common and major setback people often face when starting down the path of shadow work is an inability to be completely honest with themselves without feeling ashamed of their perceived flaws or mistakes. The ego is terrified of this work and will make itself heard once you begin, but with a loving, self-accepting attitude, you can overcome the resistance. Acknowledging your toxic traits and habits can leave you feeling raw, vulnerable, and exposed, but being willing to sit in this space is the cornerstone to all shadow work. Remember, it's perfectly okay to be imperfect. We all are. Be ready to release any shame that shows up.

Face the Darkness with Acceptance and Compassion

While radical self-acceptance sounds great, it is not always easy to embody. We must overcome shame, decisions we later regretted, and conditioned thinking that has challenged our ability to fully love ourselves. We do that with love and compassion. While it's crucial that we take full responsibility and accountability for our actions, we can do so in a gentle and loving way. Self-judgment does not support your personal development. It only creates roadblocks to healing. What we refuse to accept about ourselves will only be magnified, showing up as projected judgment toward others.

Illuminate and Challenge Your Limiting Beliefs

Illuminating the shadow means bringing awareness to where there was previously a lack of awareness. As you begin the process, you will come face to face with the conditioned thinking that birthed your most limiting beliefs. Your first instinct may be to accept those beliefs without question because this is what you have always done. The brain likes to stick to what it knows and will always choose the path with least resistance. You must be willing to confront those beliefs objectively to determine which ones are helping you and which ones are holding you back. Remember, believing something doesn't make it true.

Identify and Understand Your Triggers

I love creating content that is slightly—but safely—triggering to the people who follow my work. I don't do this to upset anyone. I do it out of love, knowing that triggers present us with the opportunity to learn and grow. It's my job to keep people thinking and exploring, even if it leaves them feeling slightly uncomfortable.

If we are identified with the ego, we may lash out or feel defensive when triggered. A big part of shadow work involves viewing our triggers as teachers, as they often lead us to exactly what needs to be addressed within us.

Acknowledge and Learn from Your Relationships

The quality of our relationships and the types of people we choose to enter into relationships with reveal a lot about what is going on in the subconscious. Someone with self-love issues may unknowingly choose to engage in relationships with people who affirm that deep-seated subconscious belief. They may attract partners and friends who are disrespectful, emotionally unavailable, and even physically or emotionally abusive. They may question why they keep repeating the same kind of people and relationships, even though they know the way they are being treated is inappropriate. Exploring the dynamics of your relationships will shed light on your own inner world.

Embrace Your Shadow for Lasting Self-Love

Approaching the shadow self with compassion and love is an absolutely essential component of shadow work. Fully accepting your shadow leads to pure and lasting self-love. The relationships we have with others are a reflection of the relationship we have with ourselves. When you have a healthy love of yourself and accept yourself as an imperfect being with gentleness, you are able to give and receive love healthily on all levels. Not only are you better able to accept others as they are, but you can also set a high standard for how you are to be loved by others. In other words, you show others how to love you by how you love yourself, and you show yourself how to better love others by embracing all parts of you with acceptance and compassion.

Find Comfort in Outside Support

Congratulations on purchasing this workbook and committing to your shadow work journey. You have an abundance of tools and resources at your disposal here, but that doesn't mean you can't also gain by seeking outside assistance. It may be helpful to find a qualified therapist who can offer support as you work through trauma. But be aware that not all therapists are trauma-informed, so if you feel that you need professional help processing your unresolved wounding, take time finding someone who is fully qualified to meet that need. A trauma-informed professional can help you cope with the discomfort of processing challenging memories.

Community support can also keep us from getting mired in the shadows as we explore the aspects of ourselves that await us there. Humans are social creatures, and the need for community has been a part of our collective story from the very beginning of time. Seeking support or social groups that are relevant to your experience can nourish your need to commune, to be seen, to feel heard, and to have space held for you. It's never been easier to connect. Thanks to advanced technology, finding your clan is a Google search away.

SET THE STAGE FOR ENGAGING WITH YOUR SHADOW

The stage you set for this work will determine its potency. Attempting to confront your shadow with a dysregulated nervous system not only will prevent you from moving forward but can actually create even more trauma. Likewise, a rigid mindset will produce resistance, leaving you feeling drained and burned out. It's a lot like trying to swim against the current—you'll use a lot of energy but won't get anywhere. Your progress is dependent on the attitude with which you go into this work.

Before diving into the second part of this book, let's explore some concepts to get you into the right mindset so you can fully use the tools being offered to you and transmute any resistance you may encounter from your ego. Having clarity on your goals and expectations will help you stay grounded and focused on the bigger picture. Your intentionality is a big step toward doing this work and setting yourself up for success.

Create a Calm and Supportive Environment

Take some time to think about your shadow work goals and how you can create the most supportive environment for meeting them. This could look like choosing to wake up an hour earlier to carve out time for self-reflection when your home is quiet. You may also choose to put on soothing music, light a candle, slip into your most comfortable PJs, or diffuse your favorite essential oils. Consider doing your work in the same place each time and creating a short ritual to soothe and settle you into a gentle space. I also recommend leaving your phone or any other distractions outside of the space.

Center Your Physical, Emotional, and Mental Self

Just as you prepare your outer environment for shadow work, it's equally important that you prepare inwardly as well. Something interesting happens in the brain when we aren't centered. The frontal cortex, which oversees logical thinking, problem-solving, and planning, becomes deactivated, and the more primal part of the brain, where the fight-or-flight response originates, becomes activated. We are reactive as opposed to responsive, and our inability to properly process uncomfortable information is greatly diminished. Take time before each shadow work session to connect to your breath and relax the muscles of the body. You may even choose a short guided mindfulness meditation to listen to before starting each time. This is a time to prepare your body, mind, and spirit.

Clarify Your Intentions

What prompted you to purchase this workbook and commit to a shadow work journey? Having clarity on your main motives will help you set realistic expectations and define your short- and long-term goals. What improvements do you wish to see? These are the types of questions you can begin asking yourself to get clear on your intentions for doing this work. It's equally important that you allow some flexibility, accepting that there is no time line to adhere to or deadlines to be met. You must also commit to allowing your journey to unfold freely and be willing to go with the flow, remaining open and curious.

Open Yourself to Deep Self-Reflection

Self-reflection is all about staying curious and remaining open to exploring possibilities that contradict what you may have always believed. It requires a commitment to consistent reevaluation as life shifts, circumstances change, and new information is attained. Taking time to mentally prepare and set intentions before starting any shadow work will help you stay in a calm, centered space, which will support the energy of self-reflection. Just remember to meet whatever shows up with gentleness and love, remaining open for the lessons that are being presented to you. There is nothing contained within your shadow that makes you unlovable. Understanding this will make self-reflection a pleasurable experience, bringing with it the opportunity for serious growth.

Dealing with Triggers and Trauma in the Moment

Triggers present us with opportunities to invite more awareness in. Our triggers lead us to what needs to be healed within. They serve as the breadcrumbs, alerting us to what needs to be addressed. The key to dealing with triggers is practicing the pause. This allows you to put space between the triggering information entering your awareness and how you will move forward based on that information. When we are reactive, we act without thinking, led primarily by the less evolved part of the brain. When we pause, we invite intentionality in, and we have a chance to decide from a more supportive state of mind how to best respond. In other words, we get to choose.

When you notice the first sign of discomfort stirring within, pause and bring your focus to the breath and body. Consciously relax the muscles, deepen the breath, and ground down. This will allow you to hold awareness around the uncomfortable emotions without becoming overly attached and overidentifying with them. Next, visualize yourself hovering over the top of your body, as if you are physically in a position that gives you a broader perspective. Begin questioning yourself from this higher perspective, asking about the feelings you are observing. Write down what is revealed in a journal for your reference.

WHAT TO EXPECT ON THE ROAD AHEAD

Each person will experience this journey differently, but one thing that remains true for all of us is that this is not a linear process. Expect twists, turns, and surprises, but also be excited for the abundance of aha moments that are sure to be had. These are the moments that will inspire you to continue forward into the unknown. Your rewards for your dedication and hard work will be greater than you can even fathom, and life will begin to unfurl in the most richly satisfying ways, making it all well worth the effort.

What awaits you along this journey I cannot say, as your path was made for you alone. What I can say, however, is that I have created the perfect companion guidebook to assist you. You will be working with affirmations to help you address mindset and reframe long-held limiting beliefs. I will also be sharing exercises to be done within the workbook and teaching you some of the same practices and techniques that I have seen clients have so much success with in my one-on-one sessions. Lastly, journal prompts will guide you through the depths of self-discovery using automatic writing.

I am thrilled and deeply honored to be your guide through this important work, and while there is sure to be some discomfort along the way, I know that the love, compassion, and acceptance of self strengthened through your commitment will be your greatest ally. You've got this!

Key Takeaways

You are well on your way to your new adventure, and I am so excited for you. We have covered a lot of information in this chapter, so before moving forward, let's recap:

- The four pillars of shadow work are self-regulation of the nervous system, mindset, radical self-love and acceptance, and forgiveness of self and others. By working with each of these concepts, you can begin to unravel the mysteries of your subconscious mind.

- Shadow work is a must for anyone who is on a journey of growth and self-discovery. While the process can be uncomfortable or even painful, the benefits it has in our lives make it worth the time and effort.

- It's important to set the stage for the work you will do in the shadows. Prepare by creating a space that is comfortable and soothing. Taking time to relax the mind through breathwork and mindfulness practices will help you stay centered and grounded.

- If this work leaves you feeling overwhelmed at any point, please seek the guidance of a trained professional such as a therapist. You can also lean into community for additional support. It's never been easier to connect with like-minded individuals.

PART II

Putting Shadow Work into Practice

Now it's time to put what you have learned into practice while I help you fill your shadow work toolbox to the brim. Each chapter in this part is focused on a specific shadow work theme. Within each of the chapters to come, you will find affirmations, exercises, practices, and journal prompts to help you better understand yourself. You can work through this part of the book from beginning to end, or you may skip around and work with the concept you feel intuitively drawn to at the time. There is no right or wrong way to access the tools included here.

Before getting started, take a moment to pause and congratulate yourself for the dedication you have shown by committing to doing this profound work. Taking action can be scary. It's much easier to stay comfortable in our same old habits and routines, even when they aren't serving us. By picking up this book, you have already demonstrated your willingness to be proactive in creating positive change in your life, and I commend you for this. While this is serious work, with the proper mindset, it can also be fun. Approaching the second part of this book with enthusiasm instead of trepidation will bring a lightness of energy to your time spent in your shadow.

CHAPTER 3

Welcome Your Shadow with Honesty and Vulnerability

"Vulnerability is the only authentic state. Being vulnerable means being open, for wounding, but also for pleasure. Being open to the wounds of life means also being open to the bounty and beauty. Don't mask or deny your vulnerability: It is your greatest asset. Be vulnerable: Quake and shake in your boots with it."

—Stephen Russell

By its very nature, vulnerability is an uncomfortable space to be in because of the fear-driven belief many of us hold that says to be vulnerable is to be weak—and to be weak opens us up to possibly being hurt. We build walls to hide our tender spaces, but in doing so we conceal our inner beauty as well. We pick and choose the parts we feel will be approved by those around us while dimming our light out of fear of judgment or criticism. When you show up to the world raw and authentic, you most certainly will not be everyone's cup of tea, but you will attract the people, situations, and experiences with which you are in alignment. In doing so, all aspects of your life will improve, and you can express your beauty fearlessly.

Vulnerability Improves Relationships

When Carlos showed up to his first session, I remember, he was anxious and noticeably uncomfortable with the one-on-one setting of trauma recovery coaching. He came to me because he felt lost, disconnected, like an outsider in his peer groups, and was plagued with social anxiety whenever he attended group functions. There weren't many people in his life outside of his younger brother and his mother, with whom he had a strained relationship. Carlos also expressed that he was lonely and that the few friendships he did have lacked any depth and meaningful connection.

After several weeks of working together, we discovered that the root issue was his fear of rejection, stemming from a childhood experience. His father had passed away when he was a teenager, and his mother, in her grieving, shut Carlos out while almost idolizing the younger brother, who strongly resembled her late husband.

This deep-seated fear made it difficult for Carlos to approach people as his true self, which caused him to come across as awkward and uncomfortable, much like he had shown up to his first session. We worked together to build back his confidence through self-love and acceptance practices, and brick by brick, Carlos started taking down the wall he had hidden behind for so many years. In time, he was able to create strong, healthy boundaries and form lasting relationships abundant in substance.

I see rejection as an opportunity for aligned redirection because I know that what is meant for me will always find me.

CONFRONTING UNCOMFORTABLE TRUTHS

Struggling to be honest and vulnerable with others is often a reflection of the internal grappling happening within the individual. Because your outer world will always mirror your inner world, self-exploration with the intention of gaining clarity is a must. This process can be very uncomfortable. This is the time you may need to lean into the radical self-acceptance I discussed in the first part of this book. Remember, no one is perfect. There is no need to feel shame about your shadow aspects. Identifying these things will help you clarify your core integral beliefs so you can consciously shift your behavior. Use the following chart to help guide you through this process.

What do I often avoid looking at within myself because it feels too uncomfortable to face?	As I bring my awareness to this particular thing, what feelings are also surfacing?	How is this avoidance mirrored in my outer world?
I feel threatened or jealous when someone has something I want for myself.	Embarrassment, shame, and discomfort	I will often judge and gossip about the person by whom I feel threatened.

CREATING POSITIVE CHANGE

Now that you have identified some of your uncomfortable truths, it's time to take steps to create positive shifts. Use this space to write a short statement of declaration that outlines what actions you will take to move through the world more aligned with your core integral beliefs. Using my previous examples, I may write, *"When I notice jealousy creeping in, I will practice being joyful for that person while also reminding myself that I, too, can have those things if I work hard and make a plan that supports my goals."*

Please read what you have written each morning and hold it in your thoughts as you move through your day. When you revisit this statement at the beginning of each day, your commitment will stay fresh in your mind, and you will have created a positive new mental habit in no time.

IDENTIFYING THE ROOT

Getting to the source of the behaviors with which you are not aligned will help you heal the root wound. What do you feel is the originating cause of your newly discovered uncomfortable truths? What has made them so difficult to look at until now? How does identifying this root wound help you be gentler and more loving toward yourself?

PROCESSING REJECTION

Because rejection is something we all must face, we need to know how to deal with it in a healthy way. Many of us have a fear of rejection. But rejection can also be seen as an opportunity for redirection, inviting us to more aligned experiences, even though it rarely feels that way in the moment. This fill-in-the-blank exercise will help you identify how you have traditionally dealt with the discomfort of rejection so that you can understand where you may need to adjust your mindset. Don't overthink your answers as you move through this exercise. Write down the first thing that comes to mind without second-guessing yourself. Bear in mind that there are no right or wrong answers.

When I experience rejection, my first reaction is usually _____ .

It often causes me to feel _____ *toward myself.*

The deepest fear I hold about rejection is _____ *, and this fear*

stems from _____

_____ .

ADOPTING A HEALTHY MINDSET ON REJECTION

Rejection no longer feels personal when you have a healthy love of self. From the space of self-acceptance, it becomes an opportunity to reevaluate and shift. Understanding this becomes easier when you embrace the idea that you want only what wants you back. Revisit this short mindfulness practice regularly to adopt a healthy mindset about rejection.

1. Find a quiet and comfortable space to sit uninterrupted, and set a ten-minute timer.

2. Close your eyes and begin focusing on the breath, deepening it with each inhalation and relaxing your muscles on the exhale.

3. Visualize yourself sitting in a bubble of white light, and set the intention of allowing your concerns and responsibilities to sit right outside of this bubble for the short time you are in this practice.

4. Begin repeating the mantra "I want only what wants me back," aloud or silently, until your timer goes off.

   You can carry this mantra with you and repeat it anytime you experience rejection to help you quickly move on.

Think about a time when you experienced a painful rejection. How did you react, and in hindsight, how did that rejection help put you on a better path? How can you choose to be thankful for the rejection you experienced?

EVALUATING PAST MISTAKES WITH LOVE, COMPASSION, AND ACCEPTANCE

We all make mistakes. When we can admit we have faltered or that we were wrong and take accountability for our actions, it allows us the space to pivot so we don't continue to make the same mistake over and over again. Use the following lines to write a short description of what you consider to be your top three mistakes. Once you are finished, read them aloud, and after each one, say the words *"I made a mistake, but I am not my mistake. I choose to love, honor, and accept myself fully."* Take a moment when you are finished to note how it feels when you choose to evaluate your past mistakes with love, compassion, and acceptance.

1. _____

2. _____

3. _____

LEARNING FROM THE PAST

Further evaluating what you consider to be your top three mistakes, ponder what you learned from each experience and how it helped you grow. You may choose to do this over several days or even weeks.

MAKING AMENDS AND TAKING ACCOUNTABILITY

One of the most vulnerable positions we can be in is admitting to someone else when we have been wrong and taking accountability for our mistakes. The fear-driven ego will resist this act, but the more you challenge yourself to be accountable for your actions, the easier it will be for you to do so. In this practice, recall when you were recently involved in a contentious situation with someone. It always takes two to tango, so when we find ourselves in these situations, we are always responsible for some aspect of the situation. Identify where you were wrong and write a letter to the other person involved, taking accountability for your part. Either present them with the letter or verbally express what you wrote. If, for some reason, it is not possible for you to do this, read the letter aloud while visualizing that you are speaking directly to the other person involved.

Begin brainstorming and drafting your letter here:

EMBRACING YOUR UNIQUENESS

According to the *Oxford Dictionary of English Etymology*, the original meaning of the Germanic word *weird* was "having the power to control destiny." From a young age, we humans tend to develop a shared fear of being thought of as different, so much so that we often hide our uniqueness from the world, allowing those parts to be witnessed only by a select few in our inner circle. And yet, when we show up to the world authentically and unapologetic about who we are, the doors of opportunity begin to fly open. We attract genuine connections, and we are free to be our fabulous selves, not allowing the fear of being judged to keep us small. In essence, we can control our destinies through our willingness to be authentic. Fill in the following blank checklist, writing down things that you feel make you unique but that you hide from others due to the fear of being thought of as weird or different. For example, do you secretly love to sing, or do you talk to yourself when you are alone? Don't worry about filling it in completely; you can add to this list as things come to you over time.

☐ _____

☐ _____

☐ _____

☐ _____

☐ _____

☐ _____

☐ _____

☐ _____

☐ _____

☐ _____

It is safe for me to be my authentic self.

BEING FEARLESSLY AUTHENTIC

Now that you have created your list of things that make you uniquely you but that you perhaps keep under wraps, it's time to practice authenticity. Choose one item at a time from your list, and commit to embracing your authenticity, allowing yourself to be witnessed in some way by others. You may choose to share something personal with someone or take some other action. For example, if you wrote down that you secretly love to sing, you may decide to do karaoke. Once you have completed the action, you can check that off your list. Challenge yourself by consistently adding to and working with your list. The more you practice, the more confident and comfortable you will be with vulnerability.

We must also allow space for others to be their unique selves without judgment, just as we embrace that for ourselves. What "weird" qualities do you judge others for, and how can you work to be more loving and accepting where this is concerned?

Key Takeaways

There are many ways we can practice being more vulnerable. Whether it's admitting our mistakes or being willing to take down our self-constructed walls, allowing ourselves to be witnessed in our rawness is the ultimate act of bravery.

- Evaluating the behaviors that don't line up with your integral belief system can be unsettling, but it's also the quickest way to get back on track and become the best version of yourself.

- An effective way of shifting your mindset around the pain of rejection is to see it as the opportunity to get back on a path more aligned with what is for your higher good. Leaning into the mantra "what is meant for me will always find me" can help you create this shift.

- We have all heard it said that it takes a big person to admit when they have been wrong. Learning to take accountability for your mistakes comfortably will facilitate your growth.

- Showing up to the world authentically is a radical act of self-acceptance that creates opportunity, improves your relationships, and facilitates a more profound sense of self-love.

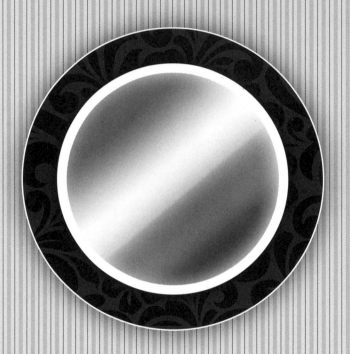

JOURNAL
PAGES

Do you view vulnerability as a strength or a weakness, and why? When you were a child, how did the adults in your life react to acts of vulnerability? How did their views affect your views as an adult?

Who do you trust enough to be vulnerable with, and why? Who don't you feel comfortable expressing this side of yourself to, and why?

How did you respond to and express your big emotions as a child? How did the adults in your life react when you expressed these emotions? What are the similarities between how you expressed and processed your heavy emotions as a child and how you do so now?

Did you feel heard as a child? How did adults respond to you when you expressed your ideas, thoughts, feelings, or concerns? How do you wish they would have responded, and how would that have made you feel? What impact has this had on you as an adult?

Psychoanalyst Carl Jung believed that the secrets of the shadow are revealed and symbolically expressed in dreams. To record your dream as soon as you wake up from it, keep this book open on this page next to your bed with a pen, and record the details of your dream here, including who was in it, what you were doing and why, and any significant objects or symbols you observed.

What do you feel the meaning of your dream is, and what do you feel its most important aspects are? What does it mirror in your waking life?

Almost everyone has at least one reoccurring dream. Write about one of yours. As you write, think about what you feel the hidden meaning of this dream might be. Trust your intuition and don't second-guess yourself during this exploration process.

The beauty of your experience is contained within the never-ending unfurling that comes with self-discovery. Your vulnerability in this work cracks you wide open in a way that allows for expansion. How do you hope to evolve as you welcome your shadow self with honesty and vulnerability?

CHAPTER 4

Face the Darkness with Acceptance and Compassion

A significant theme of this entire book is learning how to witness your shadowy aspects with a loving, compassionate, and accepting mindset. This requires exploring many layers of conditioned thinking to uncover hidden and outdated subconscious agendas. This kind of evaluation will enable you to reach a point where radical self-acceptance becomes natural.

The deep-seated shame and other subconscious narratives centered around past painful experiences will often need to be resolved before you can honestly believe yourself worthy of receiving love—from both yourself and others. Empowerment comes with being able to stand toe to toe with your shadow, armed with the energy of radical acceptance not only of yourself but of your experiences in general. Your shadow aspects provide you the most incredible opportunity for growth. Understanding this releases any resistance you may have and allows you to find a genuine appreciation for both the light and the dark that make up the whole of who you are.

In this chapter, you will be working within this concept of duality and bringing light to your dark places with loving acceptance to reduce the discomfort as you explore and integrate all parts of your being.

How Radical Self-Acceptance Helps Us Heal Our Lives

Shame and an inability to forgive yourself can lead to you feeling stuck in a loop of self-sabotaging behavior, making it difficult to embody a healthy lifestyle. This is usually because of the subconscious block that shows up in the form of a self-loathing internal narrative, constantly affirming feelings of unworthiness.

Take Elizabeth, for example. She was a victim of unresolved childhood sexual abuse. She grew into an adult who believed that there was something inherently wrong with her. She used drugs and alcohol to numb her emotional pain and to silence her intrusive thoughts, living a rock-bottom lifestyle filled with chaos and strife.

Finally, at her wits' end with the misery of her experience, she committed to exploring her childhood abuse. She began to identify how her unhealed wounding was driving her to harm herself and the people in her life who loved her. In doing so, she also had to take an honest and extremely painful look at how she had caused hurt and damage to others by attempting to numb her pain through substance abuse.

After a lot of verbal processing and self-acceptance work with Elizabeth, I created a game plan that involved cognitive behavioral therapy (CBT) to help her develop healthier thought patterns. In time, she forgave herself, which allowed her to move out of active addiction and into active healing.

THE POWER OF GRATITUDE

Without the proper perspective, you run the risk of becoming overly identified with your shadow and slipping into the victim archetype. Leaning into gratitude helps support a healthy and positive mindset that will carry you through this work. Creating a habit of feeling thankful will make it easier to process uncomfortable or traumatic experiences before the negative emotions have a chance to fester and create chaos in your subconscious. I'm not suggesting bypassing the negative emotions. Rather, it is possible to honor your experience *and* work through it simultaneously.

About a year ago, I went through an excruciating and unexpected breakup with my fiancé. Today, with plenty of time and space from that situation, I am filled with gratitude for the way things turned out. I created a lot of room for the grieving process, fully engaging with each heavy emotion that showed up, including sadness, grief, and anger. I also woke up every morning and committed to being grateful for the many things going right in my life. This daily practice kept me anchored to my higher perspective and allowed me to make healthy choices for myself while I moved through the trauma.

In this exercise, I want you to recall one of your own past painful experiences and consider how that experience benefited you in some way. Use this space to write down what comes to mind.

Even though it was really painful, I am thankful for _____

because it helped me understand _____

EMBODYING THE ENERGY OF GRATITUDE

All the clients I work with are asked to incorporate a daily gratitude practice into their routine. You should do so as well. By creating morning and evening practices centered around gratitude, you will notice that your mind naturally gravitates toward appreciation during the times in between. This is a highly transformative practice that can create true miracles.

You will want to have a dedicated notebook or journal specifically for gratitude journaling. Each morning, before you check your phone or start your day, jot down five things for which you are thankful. Detail why you are grateful for each thing and how it benefits your life. When you have finished, read each one aloud and intentionally feel as much gratitude as possible.

In the evening, right before bed, answer these questions and record the answers in your journal:

1. What were three wins that happened for me today?

2. How did abundance show up for me today?

3. What is one thing that happened today for which I am thankful?

Most of the world's population lives in such privileged societies compared to our ancestors, who bravely paved the way for so much of what we have today that makes life easy. Things like plumbing and access to food often go unnoticed, as these are just things we have come to expect will always be available. In the following space, write about something in your life you may have previously taken for granted and why you are thankful for it.

EMBRACING SELF-LOVE AS A WAY OF LIFE

Now that you have taken some time to reflect on the relationship you have with yourself, it's time to explore what self-care can look like and what activities you enjoy most. Self-love is about so much more than just self-care, but when we care for ourselves, we affirm that love through action. Incorporating self-care with your shadow work is a great way to soothe yourself through the uncomfortable emotions that are likely to come up.

Use this checklist to find inspiration, try new ways of caring for yourself, and create a more consistent self-care practice:

☐ Taking a nap

☐ Reading a book

☐ Finding a new hobby and devoting time to it consistently

☐ Creating and setting boundaries around your "me time"

☐ Saying "no" to things you don't want to do without allowing guilt to creep in

☐ Pampering yourself

☐ Spending quality time with loved ones

☐ Moving your body (e.g., through walking, yoga, or dance)

☐ Drinking more water

☐ Getting more sleep and/or creating a healthy sleep routine

☐ Taking a rest day and doing nothing

☐ Doing breathwork

☐ Meditating

☐ Soaking up some sun

☐ Doing things consistently that bring you joy

EXPLORING SELF-CARE

What does self-care mean to you, and what limiting beliefs can you identify around this subject? For example, do you feel guilty for taking time to yourself, or do you feel like there isn't enough time for rest? How much of a priority is self-care for you, and how often do you indulge yourself?

SELF-CARE IN PRACTICE

A big part of any of the work we do is putting what we have learned into practice by taking that first actionable step. Immerse yourself in self-care over this next week by committing to doing at least, but not limited to, one self-care act each day. Use the following space to plan out your seven-day self-care journey. When you have completed all seven days, evaluate how having a self-care practice affected how you feel about yourself and the world around you. Write about it in the space provided. If you thought the results were positive, I encourage you to continue with this practice.

Day One:

Day Two:

Day Three:

Day Four:

Day Five:

Day Six:

Day Seven:

I am worthy and deserving of my time
spent in self-care.

PROCESSING THE HEAVY EMOTIONS OF YOUR SHADOW WORK

Big emotions that tend to arise during the course of shadow work include guilt, grief, anger, and shame, to name just a few. Generally speaking, it's those uncomfortable feelings we'd often rather not have to feel. Avoiding challenging emotions can create a lot more suffering in the long run, so it's helpful to have a way of processing them as they show up.

It's impossible to just get over them. Sweeping them under rugs and placing our focus elsewhere doesn't make them truly go away. We must work through our feelings and learn to understand them to really release their hold over us.

When you next observe a difficult emotion, following these steps can help you process the feeling.

1. Acknowledge that the emotion is showing up. Don't try to resist it; allow yourself to experience your feeling fully.

2. Avoid judging yourself or the emotion.

3. Get curious and ask yourself why this emotion is showing up and what it is trying to show you about yourself or your current experience.

4. Reflect on what you have learned about the root cause of the heavy feeling. You may choose to do this by journaling your thoughts or talking about them with a trusted confidant.

SHADOW WORK STEPS FOR PROCESSING BIG EMOTIONS

Step 1: Engage in Nonjudgmental Observation: You experience your emotions, but you are not your emotions. There is a vast energetic difference between saying "I am angry" and saying "I feel angry." In the first scenario, you identify with the emotion, but in the second you observe the feeling and acknowledge its presence. The most important part of this step is that you don't hold any judgment. It's okay to feel your feelings, even the heavy ones.

Step 2: Identify the Originating Source: Feelings like depression, anxiety, guilt, shame, and anger are often a manifestation of a root wound, just as a fever is a symptom of a more serious underlying health issue. If you remain nonjudgmental and curious in your observation, you can begin to trace the feeling back to its source. Focusing on what triggered an emotion or when you first noticed it will shed light on its source.

Step 3: Heal the Root Wound: Once you have discovered why you are feeling the way you are, you can then begin the process of healing the originating wound. There are many ways you can do this inner work, depending on your particular issue. You will find many practices and exercises in this workbook from which you may choose, depending on your unique needs. Remember, if your wounds feel bigger than you, it's okay to ask for help. Depending on the severity of what you are working through, it may be necessary to reach out to a professional.

Step 4: Take a Break to Enjoy the Benefits of Your Hard Work: The final step is to enjoy the rewards of the hard work you have done and celebrate your healing. Don't get stuck in the shadows. This work is not meant to be done all at once. It's a lifelong process designed to help us level up in small, sustainable steps.

Shadow work has the most significant impact when it's done a little at a time as it's needed. It can be too easy to feel like the healing work is never over, and to a certain degree, there is always more healing to be done. But it must be balanced with light. Taking breaks allows what you have learned to be appropriately integrated. Your natural state is joy, love, and peace. Having worked so hard to cultivate this energy, allow yourself ample opportunities to simply enjoy it.

EXPLORING YOUR REACTION TO BIG EMOTIONS

Circle the examples that best describe how you react to big emotions.

When faced with a painful experience, I tend to:	When I am embarrassed, I tend to:	When I am angry, I tend to:
Wonder "Why me?"	Obsess	Name call
Look for the lessons	Avoid	Run away
Shut down	Hide	Shut down
Go into action	Project	Lash out
Scream	Deny	React in the moment
Vocalize	Take accountability	Pause and choose how I wish to respond
Internalize	Laugh at myself	Lose control
Cry	Self-loathe	Stay grounded

RESPONDING TO FEELINGS

How do you typically react to uncomfortable feelings when they show up? Might you choose a healthier way to confront your big emotions moving forward?

It is safe for me to fully feel my emotions. I welcome them with nonjudgment and curiosity.

CULTIVATING A HEALTHY RELATIONSHIP WITH YOURSELF

Many of us tend to be our own worst critics. Getting to a place where we can be gentle and caring with ourselves, loving the messy parts and everything in between, is a learned skill. Use this space to gauge where you may need to focus on improving the relationship you have with yourself.

List three things you love about yourself:

1. _____

2. _____

3. _____

When I thought about the three things I love about myself, I found this to be:

☐ Easy ☐ Difficult, but I was able to eventually

☐ Slightly challenging ☐ I still haven't thought of them

How do you currently feel about yourself (on a 1 to 10 scale, with 1 being not very good and 10 being excellent)?

| 1 | 2 | 3 | 4 | 5 | 6 | 7 | 8 | 9 | 10 |

What are three harsh judgments you hold against yourself?

1. _____

2. _____

3. _____

How would you describe yourself in three words?

1. _____

2. _____

3. _____

LETTING GO OF OLD IDEAS

Look back on the three harsh judgments you listed in the last exercise. What do you need to do to release those judgments? For example, do you need to forgive yourself for something? Maybe you're discovering that you are too hard on yourself. How would it change your perception of yourself if you were able to let those ideas go completely?

RELEASING JUDGMENT THROUGH THE COGNITIVE BEHAVIORAL METHOD

Many of the negative beliefs we have formed about ourselves are the results of outdated ongoing subconscious narratives that resulted from painful past experiences. Using the cognitive behavioral method, you can rewire your brain and adopt a healthier new way of thinking.

You see, the brain will always choose the path of least resistance, so if you have been thinking a certain way for a long time, it will prefer to continue thinking that way. Old thoughts become mental habits through repetition. CBT allows you to consciously reshape the way the brain thinks, creating new neural pathways. In as little as twenty-one days, you can create new automatic thought patterns. This is basically a method of choosing how you want your brain to work and then physically creating those pathways in the biological brain based on repetitive positive thinking. In my opinion, it's a little bit like magic.

Step 1: Identify the harsh thinking that creates the judgment against self.

Step 2: Create a loving thought to replace the unloving one. This should be a short mantra you can remember and repeat easily.

Use your mantra each time you notice that you are being judgmental or harsh toward yourself. Initially, you may notice that you have to use your mantra constantly, but in a very short time you will rely on it less and less because your thoughts will start to naturally gravitate toward the positivity of your mantra without conscious effort.

Key Takeaways

The relationship you have with yourself sets the tone for every other relationship in your life, which is why it's such an important topic to address. The better we can love and accept ourselves, the better we are able to give and receive love from others.

- Leaning into gratitude supports a healthy and positive mindset that will carry you through the discomfort of shadow work.

- Incorporating self-care with your shadow work is a great way to soothe yourself through the uncomfortable emotions that can come up.

- Avoiding big emotions like sadness, anger, resentment, and guilt can create a lot more suffering in the long run, which is why doing the shadow work necessary to process these emotions in a healthy way is vital.

- Being gentle and caring with ourselves is a learned skill that we must cultivate with dedication to achieve a healthy relationship with ourselves.

- Many of the negative beliefs we have about ourselves are the results of outdated and ongoing subconscious narratives that were formed as the result of painful past experiences. We can use tools such as CBT to replace them and create healthier thought patterns.

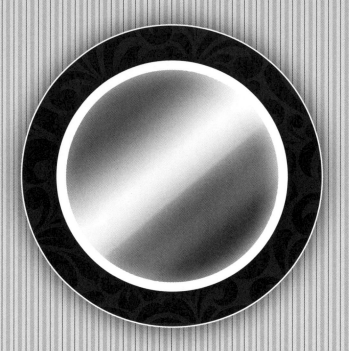

JOURNAL PAGES

Letting go of shame can be extremely challenging because it often shows up disguised as self-derogating thoughts. But holding on to shame doesn't allow space for growth. In other words, it's restrictive, not expansive. Because of shame's attachment to other uncomfortable emotions, like guilt and humiliation, the ego prefers to avoid thinking about the associated circumstances. Use the space provided to write about a shameful experience from your past, then identify the narrative you created around it.

How can you choose to release feelings of shame? Do you need to extend forgiveness to yourself? Do you need to stop taking the blame for things that weren't your fault? How can you be gentler and more compassionate with yourself? Why do you feel as if you need to hold on to these feelings?

How would it feel if you gave yourself permission to simply release the shame you formed around your past experience? How would your thinking change? Give yourself permission to grow past the shame that tethers you to a past version of yourself.

Shadow integration isn't about trying to kill your shadow. The shadow is a sacred teacher. The more love and acceptance you can extend to all aspects of your beingness, the better you are able to access the teachings from your shadow and apply the lessons learned to your life. Use this page to reflect on the things you still struggle to accept about yourself and what feelings come up around these parts of yourself.

If someone else had the traits or characteristics you wrote about on the previous page, would they make the person unlovable in your eyes? Why or why not? If not, why do you think that you can accept these things in someone else but struggle to accept them in yourself? How can you be more loving toward your imperfections?

Everything about your experience serves a higher purpose in supporting you by offering lessons that can elevate your life. Understanding this fundamental truth will help you navigate the shadows in a way that will facilitate your growth and healing. What lessons do you think your shadow can teach you? How can these facilitate growth and healing?

CHAPTER 5

Illuminate and Challenge Your Limiting Beliefs

Do not believe everything you think. A belief is nothing more than a thought that gets repeated consistently, to the point that we become attached to and identified with it. These beliefs sometimes result from conditioned thinking and can develop from past painful experiences.

We rarely have much awareness of the ongoing running narratives taking place in the depths of the unconscious mind. Still, these thoughts significantly impact our lives, creating the lens through which we view all outside experiences and affecting how we feel about ourselves, others, and the world around us. If the currents of your subconscious are self-degrading, pessimistic, or destructive, you may find yourself stuck in unhealthy patterns and feel helpless to break free. In this chapter, I will guide you to clarity by helping you dig out the underlying thoughts shaping your life—putting you back in the driver's seat through awareness and intentionality. Some of the most vital work you will do in the shadows involves illuminating your limiting beliefs and rewriting your story, which is precisely what you will learn to do in this chapter.

HOW LIMITING BELIEFS SHAPE OUR EXPERIENCES

As a mindset coach, helping people identify and address their limiting beliefs is a big chunk of the work I do with my clients. One of the most common collective blocks revolves around money, so naturally many of my clients come to me to help them sort through their conditioned thinking and adopt an abundance mindset.

Take Tracy, for example. She initially came to me because she was struggling with impostor syndrome and felt that it was keeping her from being successful in her business. For those who haven't heard this term, impostor syndrome is when we feel like a fake, which can shake our confidence and make it difficult for us to fully step into our power, keeping us small.

After spending just a few sessions together, I realized that Tracy's mindset issues went much deeper. She had a deep-rooted limiting belief that said it was selfish, greedy, and just overall bad to want money. Obviously, this mindset doesn't support someone trying to build a business. We identified this limiting belief together using a technique I created and will be sharing with you in this book. Once we got to the root cause of her impostor syndrome, we worked to shift her mindset around money, and she naturally became more confident and assured in her work. Her new perspective allowed her to finally turn a profit, and her business flourished in all areas as a result.

ILLUMINATING YOUR SUBCONSCIOUS THINKING

The first step in mindset work is to enter the role of the nonjudgmental observer of your current mindset. After all, how can you know where to begin if you don't have the needed clarity around where you currently are? Because the vast majority of our thoughts are happening outside of our conscious awareness, it can be challenging to identify precisely what is going on. Luckily, we all have a built-in tool to help us with this process.

Your emotions are the window into your subconscious mind. By observing your emotional shifts and then pausing to explore them, you can begin to bring light to the murky aspects of your subconscious. Spend at least one week observing and recording your observations. Doing so will help you quickly recognize any common themes or patterns. Remain nonjudgmental and approach this exercise with curiosity. You will be working with three core questions to explore your emotional state.

Use the following worksheet to help guide you through the process. You may want to continue this work in a journal, as you will likely have several entries in a day. Don't worry about changing or adjusting your mindset at this time. Right now, it's just about observing and nothing more.

What is the observed emotional shift?	What external factors, if any, contributed?	What were the thoughts you had as the shift happened?

REWRITING YOUR STORY

Don't begin the second step in this process unless you have spent at least a week paying attention to your emotional shifts and recording them. Once this is completed, you should have a clear picture of where you need to focus your attention. The next step is to rewrite your story, creating a new narrative that serves and supports you. Process each narrative one at a time, allowing space so that your new story can be fully integrated. This ongoing process may take several weeks or even months to work through.

What is the limiting belief or unhealthy narrative you discovered?

Example: *Tracy's limiting belief was that money was the root of all evil and that it was wrong of her to want to attract more of it through her work.*

Now it's time to rewrite your story. Read over what you have written regularly to integrate your new narrative into the subconscious mind.

Example: *The new story Tracy and I worked together to create stated that she deserved to be supported in her work so she could help even more people, and that she needed to have her needs met so that she could show up for her clients in a healthy way. We also created a narrative that said it was good for her to have money because she used it positively, which benefited her, her family, her clients, and her community.*

I choose to witness my thoughts with love, acceptance, and curiosity in the absence of judgment.

GROWTH MINDSET VERSUS FIXED MINDSET

Individuals who possess a growth mindset generally believe that they can improve upon any skill they wish with time and effort. They tend to see failure as an opportunity for growth and understand the importance of consistency and determination in reaching their goals. In addition to these qualities, those who have adopted a growth mindset are open to exploration and contemplate new ideas and concepts as they are presented.

The opposite of a growth mindset is a fixed mindset. Individuals with a fixed mindset hold a limiting belief that they can't move beyond their circumstance to a more desired outcome, which stunts their developmental process.

Most of us fall somewhere in the gray area between these two extremes. This exercise will help you get a clear idea of how open or fixed your mindset is. Circle the following statements that *best* describe your current thinking.

Growth Mindset	Fixed Mindset
I believe mistakes are an opportunity to learn and adjust.	I feel discouraged, and sometimes even ashamed, when I make a mistake.
I enjoy being challenged.	I find challenges overwhelming and try to avoid complex tasks and goal-setting.
Witnessing others' success inspires me.	I feel threatened and sometimes even jealous when others succeed.
I am open to considering new ideas that may contradict my current belief system.	Being right is important to me, and I am not open to considering contradicting views.
I welcome constructive criticism.	I am easily offended by constructive criticism.
I enjoy tackling complicated projects and tend to set lofty goals for myself.	I tend to avoid situations that I am unsure of or not knowledgeable about.
I've been knocked down my share of times, but I always get back up and keep pushing forward.	I abandon projects or give up easily on my goals if I feel I am not making progress.
I can motivate myself easily.	I need validation from others to stay motivated.
When something doesn't work out how I had hoped, I can be flexible and develop creative solutions.	When things don't work out the way I had hoped, I tend to give up.

A LESSON LEARNED

Use this space to write about a past mistake you made. What lesson did you learn from this experience, and how has it helped you move forward with a different perspective?

EMBRACING CHALLENGE

This practice will help you cultivate a growth mindset by actively seeking out challenges in your life. Commit to one new challenge or set one new goal per week for the next six weeks. At the beginning of each week, choose what this will be and write it in the space provided.

Challenge

Week 1

Week 2

Week 3

Week 4

Week 5

Week 6

*I welcome challenge as an opportunity
for growth.*

WORKING WITH YOUR EGO

At the root of our limiting beliefs is the fearful voice of the ego. Building a solid relationship with your ego while learning to soothe and comfort it will help break down limiting beliefs organically and lovingly. But first, you must gain clarity by identifying your fears. Use this space to write about or draw your most common fears (e.g., fear of being rejected or fear of failure).

THREE STEPS TO SOOTHE THE EGO

You will want to call upon this practice when you feel triggered, rejected, competitive, unworthy, emotionally needy, or judgmental of others.

Step 1: Acknowledge the ego with love and identify the message your ego is sending through your triggered response.

Example: *I feel angry and embarrassed that I was passed over for a promotion that I worked very hard to get. I feel jealous of the coworker who got the promotion instead and feel they aren't nearly as qualified as I am for the position.*

Step 2: Address the root fear by asking your ego why it is afraid.

Example: *I feel fearful that I am not good enough at my job and worry that I may never get another chance to move up.*

Step 3: Reassure your ego.

Example: *I know that this is disappointing, but this isn't a reflection of my worthiness. What is meant for me will always find me, so I can let this go knowing there is something better in store.*

REFRAMING LIMITING STATEMENTS

How we express ourselves outwardly is a good indication of our inner dialogue. For example, someone who regularly states that they can't do something may have a limiting opinion around their ability to achieve. Or someone who makes sarcastic jokes at their own expense may have a deep-seated belief about their self-worth. Examining the tone of your speech and the words with which you choose to express yourself is a wonderful tool to identify hidden limiting beliefs. Here you will find a list of limiting statements. Use the space beside each to write a more positive reframing statement.

Limiting Statement	Reframing Statement
Example: I can't . . .	*Example: Anything is possible with work, a good plan, and dedication.*
Why bother? What's the point?	
Who cares?	
I hate . . .	

Limiting Statement	Reframing Statement
I'm so over it!	
It's too hard . . .	
There isn't enough time. I can't catch up.	
Life is difficult . . .	

YOUR INNER NARRATIVE

What are some of your most common limiting statements, and how do they reflect your inner narrative? How can you reframe those statements to something more helpful?

POSITIVE STATEMENT MEDITATION

The first step in this process is to quiet your internal chatter through breathwork. Set a timer for three to five minutes and follow these breathwork instructions to begin.

Inhale through your nose for a count of five seconds and then slowly exhale through your nose for a count of six seconds. Extending your exhale in this way signals the brain to slow down and calms the nervous system.

Once you have done a few minutes of this breathing and feel calm and content, begin repeating a stream of positive statements in your head or aloud. Use some of the following or create your own:

- Life is easy when I allow it to be.

- I love and value myself.

- I am worthy of all that I desire.

- I can accomplish anything I set my mind to.

- What is meant for me will always find me.

- I am happy with where I am and excited to see where I am headed.

- I have so much to be thankful for.

- Life is beautiful when I am willing to witness it in this way.

- I am the creator of my experience.

- There is so much goodness in the world.

- I trust in the virtue of others.

- I am fully supported.

- _____

- _____

- _____

- _____

- _____

Key Takeaways

Illuminating and confronting your limiting beliefs is a lifelong process, as new ideas are formed from our past and present experiences. Here are some of the key points discussed in this chapter:

- The first step in mindset work is always the nonjudgmental observation of the current mindset. This self-evaluation will bring attention to what needs to be addressed within.

- Your emotions are the window into your subconscious mind. By observing your emotional shifts and then pausing to explore them, you can identify the underlying thoughts associated with them.

- Those with a fixed mindset hold a limiting belief that they can't move beyond their current circumstances and thinking patterns.

- Individuals with a growth mindset generally believe that they can improve upon any skill they wish with time and effort.

- At the root of our limiting beliefs is the fearful voice of the ego. Building a solid relationship with your ego will help break down limiting beliefs.

- How we express ourselves outwardly is a good indication of our inner dialogue. Examining the tone of your speech and the words you choose to express yourself will help you identify hidden limiting beliefs.

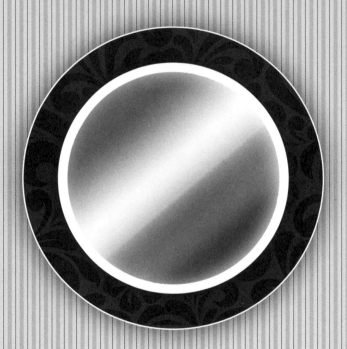

JOURNAL PAGES

Naming the ego can help you observe it while not becoming identified with it. The ego is often villainized, but in truth, the ego has made it possible for humans to survive as a species. So, really, you should be grateful for that little nagging voice that aims to keep you safe. The ego has only the best intentions for you, but it's up to you to set boundaries and reassure it that you can make safe and healthy choices. In this exercise, write a reassuring and loving letter to your ego.

Dear _____ (name of your ego),

Thank you for always wanting to keep me safe. I understand that you are concerned

about _____

_____

_____ ,

but I want you to know that (fill in the remaining lines with a reassuring and loving

message to your ego) _____

_____

_____

_____

_____ .

Sincerely,

_____ (Your Name)

The ego likes to use comparison as a tool for reassurance, which often takes root as feelings of not being good enough or unworthiness. How often do you find yourself identified with this type of narrative? Do you need external validation to feel worthy or good about yourself? What is the underlying fear?

The ego can be activated by challenges from others. How do you most commonly react when others challenge you? Is it difficult to witness an opinion that differs from your own without speaking up against it or challenging the person who is expressing it? What is your underlying fear?

Identify a toxic cycle in your life. When did this cycle begin? How does it have a negative impact on your life? What perceived benefit does this cycle offer you? Is it instant gratification? Does it help you numb uncomfortable feelings? Does it give you a burst of excitement?

A person who feels like they must drink to be social may believe that they aren't as funny sober and that people won't like them as much. Because of that belief, they may continue to overdrink in social situations. This is an example of how limiting beliefs keep us stuck in unhealthy cycles. Looking at the toxic cycle you identified in the previous prompt, what limiting belief is fueling the cycle?

What are some of the most persistent toxic thoughts in your life? Do they create discomfort in the body? If so, where and how? Do they create mental discomfort, like anxiety or depression?

What fear, grief, or trauma has created your most common toxic thoughts? What is a new story you can create around them? Use the space provided to reframe these negative thoughts by rewriting your story. For example, if you were told you weren't good enough at some point, and you created a story that affirmed that, reframe that story by writing down all the ways in which you are good enough.

Write down three of your most limiting beliefs along with positive mantras you can replace them with. For example, if you have a belief, "I am not good enough to be in a leadership position," you might replace this with the mantra, "I trust that I can be good in any role I dedicate myself to." When you are done, use these mantras as your old beliefs show up in your daily life.

CHAPTER 6

Identify and Understand Your Triggers

An uncomfortable truth many have a difficult time with is that our triggers reflect our inner wounding, leading us to what needs to be healed. While it's easier to blame others for how we feel or for our reactions, we are solely responsible for both. For example, someone can't make you mad. They may do something that you find displeasing, but you decide if you will react or respond and what that looks like. When we allow others to dictate these things, we give our power away and are at the mercy of outside forces. The only behavior any of us can control is our own. So often, we subconsciously try to manage those around us so that they behave in a way we find pleasing, and when they disappoint us by acting differently, we end up feeling triggered.

In this chapter, you will be working with your triggering to uncover your hidden wounds and learn how to use them as a powerful tool to deepen your understanding of yourself. In time and with practice, you will begin to heal your triggers by understanding their root cause.

Healing Triggers
Leads to Resolution

Kathy was a self-proclaimed control freak and was thought of this way by friends, coworkers, and her three adult children. Time spent with her family, especially her grandchildren, was very important to her, and she loved inviting everyone over on Sundays for a big family meal. Still, at the end of the evening, she often felt triggered, which showed up as frustration and disappointment. You see, Kathy always held expectations of how she wanted the day to go. She would envision the grandkids running around in the backyard while the men watched football and the women helped her in the kitchen. Things rarely went as she wished.

When she shared her frustrations and hurt feelings with me, I asked why it was so important that she have so much control over these family gatherings. She shared that she felt guilt about the fact that her children did not have a present father for a big chunk of their childhood as the result of divorce. She had such fond memories of her own father and how her home had been run, and she desperately wanted to give that to her own children. Controlling family members' behavior during these family gatherings was her way of trying to create for them her picture-perfect vision of what such gatherings should be like. Once we pinpointed the cause of her need to control, she was able to resolve her guilt and allow family gatherings to unfold without being attached to an outcome.

EXPLORING YOUR MOST COMMON TRIGGERS

There is a space available between the moment of triggering and your response if you choose to allow it. Unfortunately, because the emotions invoked when we feel triggered can be so intense, many of us don't take advantage of this precious time and lash out or act impulsively, led by reactionary energy. Such reactions lead to feelings of guilt or shame if we have acted outside of our integral beliefs. Practicing the pause when you are triggered creates the space for you to move away from reactiveness and into responsiveness. Let's explore some of your most common triggers, beginning with observation.

Triggering Situations or Content	How Trigger Manifested	Notes
	☐ Anger ☐ Guilt ☐ Shame ☐ Frustration ☐ Sadness ☐ Anxiety ☐ _____	
	☐ Anger ☐ Guilt ☐ Shame ☐ Frustration ☐ Sadness ☐ Anxiety ☐ _____	
	☐ Anger ☐ Guilt ☐ Shame ☐ Frustration ☐ Sadness ☐ Anxiety ☐ _____	

PRACTICING SELF-REGULATION TO BECOME LESS REACTIVE

When the nervous system is dysregulated, we are more easily triggered. Learning self-regulation helps you become less reactive. A dysregulated nervous system means that the most primal part of the brain, where the fight-or-flight response originates, is activated. When we bring the nervous system back into regulation, we shut that part off, allowing the frontal lobes, which are responsible for logic, planning, and decision-making, to take over.

Self-regulation is easy to do but requires consistency to become a habit. We can control what parts of the brain are activated by controlling our muscles. Try checking in with your body five to ten times a day by doing a body scan. Starting at the top of the head, move your awareness down the body, observing where you are tensing and then intentionally relaxing those muscles. Stick with this practice for at least three weeks to build the habit. Take note of how you feel before self-regulation and after.

How do you most commonly react to being triggered? Understanding your common reactions will help you break unhealthy cycles. What situation have you recently been triggered by and how did you handle it? Is there a better way you could have responded? What would that have been?

CREATE A PLAN TO HELP YOU PRACTICE THE PAUSE

Having a plan for how you will handle triggering before you are confronted with triggers will help you become less reactive. For example, you may choose to remove yourself and cool off before deciding how to move forward or practice deep breathing to soothe the uncomfortable emotions showing up. Use this space to determine how you will choose to respond in these situations as they arise.

What triggers do you feel are the most difficult to let go of, and why do you feel that is? How do they relate to your past traumas?

I remain in control of my actions by choosing to be responsive.

USING YOUR SENSES TO GROUND YOU WHEN TRIGGERED

Grounding is a technique used to bring us back into our physical body and away from identifying with our heavy emotions. This practice works best when you feel angry, scattered, or anxious.

Next time you are experiencing triggering, pause and identify the following:

- Five things you can see

- Four things you can touch

- Three things you can hear

- Two things you can smell

- One thing you can taste

How does triggering feel in your physical body? Does it cause your heart to race, your throat to tighten, or your hands to clench? Knowing how these emotions settle in your body will help identify how you store them and allow you to safely release that energy.

TRACING YOUR TRIGGERS BACK TO THE ORIGINATING SOURCE

When you take time to explore the origin of your triggers, you can heal them at the source. Refer to the first exercise in this chapter, where you identified your most common triggers. Work through your list, one item at a time. Use the questions that follow to trace your triggers back to their originating source.

What is the triggering situation?

Example: *I feel triggered when I see people dancing on social media.*

What emotions do you experience around this trigger?

Example: *I feel annoyed and even angry sometimes.*

Why do you think you experience these feelings from this particular situation?

Example: *I wish I also had the confidence to show up authentically and unconcerned with what others may think, so I feel jealous when I see others able to be present so freely.*

What previous experience did this trigger stem from?

Example: *As a child, I was often told that I was too much. This constant message made me feel weird or different and caused me to have insecurities. I grew to fear what people may think of me if I expressed this side of myself.*

My triggers are my greatest teacher,
leading me to what needs to be healed
within myself.

TESTING YOUR TRIGGERS

Healthy triggering pushes people outside of their comfort zone and will often get them thinking. When we challenge ourselves to allow triggers to teach us, we build metaphorical muscles and become less easily triggered. Challenge yourself by intentionally putting yourself in a triggering situation while practicing some of the tools laid out for you in this chapter. Use this space to write about your experience.

What were the biggest challenges you faced when you intentionally confronted triggering situations or content, and what tools worked best for helping you cope?

EXTENDING COMPASSION

Many of our triggers revolve around others' behavior and how we perceive their actions, often taking them personally. When we practice being compassionate, we naturally become less bothered by the behavior of others. The truth is, very rarely are the actions of others explicitly against us. For example, someone who was short with you on the phone may have been worried about their sick child and anxious to get back to caring for them. This next exercise and the following practice will help you embrace a more compassionate attitude toward others.

List three people who often trigger you. Include notes on why and how you experience these triggers.

1. _____

2. _____

3. _____

CONNECTING TO COMPASSION THROUGH METTA MEDITATION

Metta meditation, otherwise known as loving-kindness meditation, can be challenging if we have built-up resentment or anger from being consistently triggered by a specific individual. Choose one of the people you listed in the previous exercise. Next, find a comfortable space where you won't be interrupted. Close your eyes, relax your body, and focus on your breath to center yourself. Once you feel calm, bring the person about whom you will be meditating to mind. Repeat the following statements five times in the order they are written. This is a powerful practice that will bring you home to love.

- I send _____ [name of the person] love.

- I wish _____ [name of the person] peace.

- I wish _____ [name of the person] joy.

- I wish _____ [name of the person] abundance and prosperity.

- I choose to love and accept _____ [name of the person].

Key Takeaways

Hopefully, you have a new appreciation for the people, content, and situations that activate your heavy emotions. Now it is time for you to enjoy your newfound confidence in confronting your triggers. Remember, the more you engage these triggers, the better you will become at healthily processing and healing them. Here is a brief summary of what we covered in this chapter:

- Your triggers are guiding you to what needs to be healed within yourself. Approaching them with curiosity will help you overcome them.

- When the nervous system is dysregulated, you feel more triggered. By practicing self-regulation, you automatically become less reactive. The best way to do this is by focusing on the body's muscles and intentionally relaxing where you are holding tension.

- It's essential to have a plan for how you will choose to deal with triggering content, people, or situations. Doing so helps you become less reactive and more responsive.

- When you take time to explore the originating source of your triggers, you can heal them at the source.

- Many of our triggers revolve around the behavior of others and how we judge their actions. When we practice being compassionate, we naturally become less bothered by others' behavior.

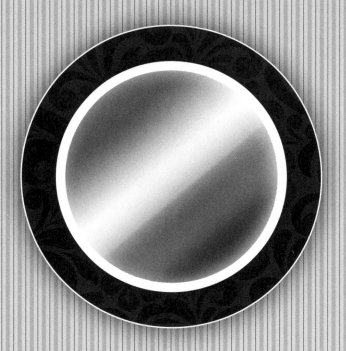

JOURNAL
PAGES

You become disempowered when you give your energy away to your past experiences and other triggering situations that surface in your day-to-day life. You may be totally unaware of the ways in which you give your energy away. I say *give* because your energy can't be taken from you. It's a choice being made either on a conscious or subconscious level. Repeat this mantra while breathing your energy back into your body, and then use the space that follows to create other empowering mantras and affirmations you can call upon as needed.

"I now choose to call back to me any energy that I have consciously or unconsciously given away."

Empowerment to me means _____
_____ ,

and I feel most empowered when _____
_____ .

I observe that I feel disempowered when I am experiencing big emotions such as
_____
_____ ,

and I tend to react to this by _____
_____ .

A more empowering way to respond would be to _____
_____ .

Recall a time when something uncomfortable or upsetting showed up for you.
What were the circumstances, and did you react in a way that left you feeling
empowered or disempowered? Is there a way you might choose to respond next
time that feels more aligned to you?

_____
_____
_____
_____
_____
_____
_____
_____

Choose one trigger you wish to work with from the previous exercise and take a moment to think back to when you first started being reactive toward that particular person, place, thing, content, or situation. What is the root cause of the trigger? Once you have identified the root cause, write about the experience.

What is your most common reaction when you feel emotionally triggered? Do you lash out in anger? Do you say things you don't mean? Do you retreat and shut down? Or do you deny the uncomfortable emotion and bottle it up? These are just some examples, but identifying how you react will help bring more awareness to these cycles.

I recommend practicing self-regulation before and during any shadow work so that you are grounded and in a centered state of mind while addressing uncomfortable and triggering topics. Top-down methods of regulating the nervous system aim to quiet the mind to relax the body, but a bottom-up approach aims to first relax the body to calm the mind. To practice the bottom-up method of self-regulation, simply become aware of tension in the body and relax the corresponding muscles. Use the following checklist to move through the body and identify areas where you are tense. Some signs that you are holding tension include a clenched jaw, sucking in the belly, furrowed brows, and balled-up hands.

☐ Crown of the head   ☐ Upper abdomen

☐ Forehead   ☐ Lower abdomen

☐ Behind the eyes   ☐ Buttocks

☐ Jaw   ☐ Thighs

☐ Neck   ☐ Calves

☐ Shoulders   ☐ Hands

☐ Upper back   ☐ Feet

☐ Lower back

Before you address any tensions, think about how you're feeling about your mental clarity and emotional well-being. Rate each on a scale of one to ten, with one being the best and ten being the worst. Do not overthink your answers, but rather, instinctively jot down the first number that comes to mind.

Mental Clarity: _____

Emotional Well-Being: _____

Now, take a few deep breaths and bring your focus to releasing tension in the areas you identified using the checklist. Breathe in a relaxed energy, focusing on melting away the tension in those muscles for one full minute. Afterward, rate how you feel again using the same scale of one to ten. Record any thoughts and feelings about the difference before and after self-regulating.

Mental Clarity: _____

Emotional Well-Being: _____

_____

_____

_____

_____

_____

_____

_____

_____

_____

_____

_____

CHAPTER 7

IMPROVE YOUR RELATIONSHIPS THROUGH SHADOW WORK

While we may think of shadow work mostly as a means for healing trauma and confronting our limiting beliefs, part of this work is also about examining our attitudes and thinking around the important relationships in our life. When you commit to doing the inner work, your life improves in all areas. As you learn to embrace radical self-acceptance, you can readily accept others with love and compassion as well.

While many relationships will improve through your dedication to your inner work, some may also fall away. The more confident and comfortable you are at creating healthy boundaries, the more discerning you will be where your relationships are concerned. Those who are meant to be in your life will honor your newfound self-love, but do expect some initial resistance to the healthy boundaries you create for yourself.

In this chapter, you will be exploring your relationship patterns and behaviors. You will be examining their quality and taking an honest and often uncomfortable look at how your shadow affects your most valued connections with family, friends, lovers, and acquaintances.

People-Pleasing: A Trauma Response

People-pleasing tendencies are a typical trauma response among those who have suffered childhood trauma. This doesn't mean just abuse or neglect. Many times, childhood trauma is far more subtle. Take Emily, who grew up in a home where her parents spent much time rehashing their ongoing relationship dramas. Starting at a very young age, Emily's mother would often depend on her for the emotional support she didn't receive from her husband, placing unrealistic expectations on Emily to behave in a way that her mother found pleasing.

As Emily grew and formed other relationships, she carried the people-pleasing tendencies taught to her by the dynamic she had with her mother into adulthood. She became somewhat of a chameleon, her personality changing depending on whom she spent time with. Her fear of how others would receive her made it difficult for her to show up authentically. She allowed the opinions of the people in her life to impact her feelings of self-worth, creating a cycle in her romantic relationships that left her feeling empty and lost.

In my time with her, we focused heavily on inner child work and reparenting. For the first time in her life, Emily felt confident enough to be her fabulous self. She was finally set free.

CODEPENDENCY ASSESSMENT WORKSHEET

The definition of codependency, according to the Merriam-Webster dictionary, is "a psychological condition or a relationship in which a person manifesting low self-esteem and a strong desire for approval has an unhealthy attachment to another often controlling or manipulative person (such as a person with an addiction to alcohol or drugs)."

Like other shadow aspects, many people are entirely unaware of their own codependent tendencies. Even though codependency is sometimes referred to as relationship addiction and is often thought of in connection with romance, this unhealthy and often one-sided attachment can form around any relationship. While it's true that these toxic bonds are often created when one person is in need of being "fixed," that certainly isn't always the case.

There are many other root causes of codependency that can create the unhealthy need for approval, love, attention, and acceptance from a particular person or people in our life. Use the following worksheet to assess if you are engaging in codependent tendencies. Take time to carefully consider the options listed here and contemplate which statements *best* resemble your thoughts, actions, and views.

CONTINUED >

Codependency Assessment Worksheet continued

Healthy Relationship Mindset	Codependent Relationship Mindset
☐ I can easily express myself, even when I feel it may disappoint or upset others.	☐ I often downplay how I feel and have difficulty sharing my thoughts, ideas, or opinions, especially if I know others may not receive them well.
☐ I create and enforce healthy boundaries and understand that everyone is responsible for their behavior and choices.	☐ I believe when you love someone, you never give up on them.
☐ I prioritize my needs knowing this helps me healthily serve others.	☐ I put others' needs ahead of my own and am devoted to being of service, even if it means self-sacrifice.
☐ I understand I may not be everyone's cup of tea, and that's okay.	☐ It's important that others like me.
☐ While I don't enjoy confrontation, I am not afraid to stand up for what is right, even if it means that I upset or disappoint others.	☐ I avoid confrontation, even if it means going against my core values and beliefs at times.
☐ I can easily say "no" if I feel it is in my best interest.	☐ I have a difficult time saying "no" and will often do things just to please others.
☐ While I enjoy being of service, each person is responsible for caring for their needs.	☐ It's important for me to feel needed by those in my life.
☐ I apologize only if it is sincere and if I have done something in error.	☐ I often find myself apologizing even when I've done nothing wrong.

OBSERVING HEALTHY RELATIONSHIPS

Being in observation of other relationships is an ongoing practice that will help you identify healthy and unhealthy behaviors, enabling you to pinpoint unhealthy relationship behaviors in yourself.

Think of some of the people in your life who are in happy and balanced relationships. Use the checklist from the previous exercise to bring clarity to what a healthy relationship mindset looks like.

Once you have identified these things, begin observing how the people involved in these relationships move, speak, and interact with one another. Note their healthy habits and the benefits these habits have for their relationship.

If you feel close to and comfortable with these people, sit down and talk with them. Ask how they handle conflict, what boundaries they have created, and what social activities and hobbies they enjoy outside of their relationship. Use these questions as a starting point for yourself and add to these as you feel called.

Most of us have exhibited codependent tendencies at some point in our life. Identify a time you fell into this pattern. How did you feel, and what difficulty did you have expressing your feelings? What were the root fears that caused you to slip into codependent behavior?

GETTING CLEAR ON YOUR BOUNDARIES

We hear a lot about the need to create and enforce healthy boundaries, but the truth is many people don't have clear-cut and decided-upon boundaries to implement. When there is a lack of clarity around this, boundaries become confusing and are often weak or not established.

While guiding you through this exercise, I offer things for you to consider, but take time to contemplate your boundaries past the examples shared here. There are five main areas you will focus on. Use this worksheet to clarify and define your boundaries within each.

1. **Define your physical boundaries.** How do you feel about public displays of affection? Is it okay for your partner to give you nonsexual affection without permission, or do you like to be the one to invite this type of physical contact? Are there times you prefer not to be bothered, such as when you are in the bathroom or working? How much alone time do you need to feel your best?

2. **Define your sexual boundaries.** Are there things that are off-limits for you sexually? With whom do you feel comfortable engaging in sexual acts, and under what conditions? For example, do you need to be in love, or are you comfortable having sex on a first date? What do you need to feel comfortable and confident with your sexual partner? Is monogamy important to you, or do you have a less conventional view on what constitutes a healthy relationship?

3. **Define your boundaries around money.** Do you feel comfortable loaning money to or borrowing money from friends or family? Are there people to whom you do not wish to lend money, and why? Do you want to keep your money separate from your partner, or do you like sharing a joint account? Who pays for what?

4. **Define your emotional boundaries.** Do you feel your feelings are heard and validated? Do you feel you can express yourself without being criticized or judged? Can you convey to others when you feel uncomfortable discussing certain topics, and what are those specific topics?

5. **Define your time boundaries.** Is it essential for you to have time outside of your romantic relationships, and what does this look like for you? What goals do you have that require your time? How much time do you need with your friends, family, and romantic partners to feel nourished within the relationships? Is it easy for you to say "no" to requests made on your time when what is asked doesn't feel like something you want to do?

ESTABLISHING AND ENFORCING NEEDED BOUNDARIES

Now that you have gotten clear, written out your boundaries in the five key areas, and identified where you need to strengthen these boundaries with the people in your life, it's time to apply this information. This may require you to discuss your needs and expectations with a partner, family members, and friends.

As you begin enforcing new boundaries, be prepared for some initial turbulence in your relationships. After all, no one likes change, and to some, boundaries can feel like rejection or abandonment. Aim to create healthy expectations in your life without being harsh. As everyone adjusts, your relationship with yourself and others will be significantly improved through your dedication to holding firm boundaries in these key areas of your life.

"Sometimes you are the toxic person. Sometimes you are the mean, negative person you're looking to push away. Sometimes the problem is you. And that doesn't make you less worthy. Keep on growing."

—Unknown

MAKING HEALTHY CHANGES

With the clarity you now have around your important boundaries, what healthy changes can you make in your life? How will you commit to your set boundaries? What fears do you have around setting and holding these boundaries?

I easily create and hold boundaries that honor and support my core values.

CONFRONTING YOUR TOXIC RELATIONSHIP HABITS: ARE YOU THE PROBLEM?

Taking accountability is a powerful shadow work lesson presented to all of us from time to time. When issues arise in your relationships, the ego, in its attempt to keep you safe, will try to convince you that it is all the fault of the other person or people involved. The truth is, it always takes two to tango, and if your relationships are strained, acknowledge that you are participating, on some level, in whatever is straining them.

Work through this exercise by checking off the response that best describes your tendencies in each situation. Then write a short mission statement explaining how you plan on adjusting your behavior, if needed.

An example of your mission statement might be: *"When I am given constructive criticism, I will pause and consider whether what is offered is accurate and valuable. I will be open to receiving this information without becoming defensive."*

When I receive constructive criticism, my most common response is to:

☐ Shut down because of embarrassment or shame.

☐ Go into attack mode and deflect onto the other person.

☐ Cry, yell, guilt, or throw fits. (Behavior like this is an attempt to emotionally manipulate the other person into behaving differently.)

☐ None of the above. I am open to receiving guidance and constructive criticism from others, and I have set clear boundaries around what I am and am not comfortable discussing at the time.

The next time I receive constructive criticism, I intend to (add your mission statement):

_____

_____

_____

_____

CONTINUED→

Confronting Your Toxic Relationship Habits:
Are You the Problem? continued

When I feel like the person I care about isn't giving me enough time, I:

☐ Withhold, pout, or exhibit passive-aggressive behavior to gain their attention by showing them that I am upset.

☐ Try to control and dictate their behavior by insisting they yield to my wants around their time.

☐ Feel rejected and internalize their behavior, often feeling sorry for myself or insecure about the relationship. (Depression and jealousy are common experiences for those who commonly fall into this mindset trap.)

☐ None of the above. I take time to contemplate my feelings and then express myself about where I may require some extra love and support.

The next time I feel as if I need more time from my partner, family member, or friend, I will respond by:

_____

_____

_____

When it comes to being honest:

☐ I will lie in my relationships if I feel it will avoid conflict or if I feel the truth will negatively impact me.

☐ I don't make a habit of lying, but an occasional white lie never hurt anyone.

☐ My mistrust of others makes it difficult for me to express myself candidly.

☐ None of the above. While I may fall short, I value the importance of honesty and strive to be as truthful as I can. I understand that honesty, combined with healthy communication, is vital for the health of any relationship.

I commit to being more truthful and honest by:

_____

_____

_____

_____

When it comes to dealing with others, I:

☐ Can be very critical and become frustrated or angry when someone doesn't adjust their behavior based on my opinions.

☐ Tend to project my frustrations on those I'm closest with, even when they aren't the cause of my aggravation. (This often happens when a person is overwhelmed and needs a release of energy.)

☐ Let them take the lead and try not to rock the boat in an attempt to keep the peace.

☐ None of the above. I strive to honor both myself and those I have in my life. I am discerning about my relationships, always striving to create healthy bonds.

I commit to improving my relationships through my actions by:

_____

_____

_____

_____

_____

_____

_____

_____

The more I can love, honor, and accept myself, the easier it is for me to love, honor, and accept others.

ACCOUNTABILITY PRACTICE

There is something liberating about taking accountability when we have stumbled or behaved outside of our core values within our relationships. Make a list of times when you have been in this situation and focus on them one at a time. Notice what emotions show up as you confront your past mistakes and relationships slipups. Acknowledge your part in the disagreement or strife between you and each person involved. Then forgive yourself and commit to choosing better in the future.

RELATIONSHIPS AS YOUR MIRROR

Our closest connections with others serve as a valuable tool for self-discovery when we open up to the understanding that relationships are mirrors. For example, an individual who fears receiving love may subconsciously choose partners who are emotionally unavailable, all the while wondering why they seem to keep attracting this same type of person.

In this exercise, you will be taking a closer look at what your relationships are mirroring about your subconscious beliefs. Reflect upon each type of relationship and open yourself up to consider what they mirror back to you about yourself. Write a short description for each in the boxes.

Romantic Relationships (Past, Present, or Both)	Parental Relationship	Siblings/Other Family Members	Friendships

REFLECTION MEDITATION

This meditation is a simple visualization exercise that is easy to memorize. Use it whenever you want to connect with your inner self for clarity. You may go into this meditation open to receiving whatever message needs to come through, or you might have a specific question you would like answered. Make sure to have a journal handy to write down your experience when you are finished.

To begin, find a comfortable space where you won't be disturbed. You may choose to sit or lie down. I also recommend putting on some gentle meditation music to help you relax. Next, focus on your breath, deepening your inhalation and releasing tension with the exhalation. Allow your body to relax completely.

Once you are in a relaxed body and mind, visualize a path before you that leads into an ancient forest. As you travel the trail, allow the details of this scene to unfold for you. You may hear birds chirping or notice other small forest creatures scurrying around. Notice how comforted and safe you feel as you go deeper into the woods.

As you continue on your path, you notice a small body of water in the distance. You move toward it until you are at the water's edge. At first the water is choppy, and waves on the surface make it difficult to see anything being reflected.

Call your question or intention to the front of your mind now while kneeling by the water. As your question or intention moves into focus, the water becomes smoother, until it is perfectly still. As you gaze down upon your own image on the surface of the crystal-clear water, ask for a message or pose your question. Allow your reflection to speak to you, and listen intently to the message. You may sit here and engage in conversation, asking and then receiving, for as long as you like. When you are finished, write down the messages you received and reflect upon their meaning.

EXPLORING YOUR PATTERNS

What common patterns can you identify among your closest relationships? Which are healthy, and which do you feel need your attention? What is the underlying narrative of each?

Key Takeaways

You are now on the road to having a clear picture of the inner workings of your most special bonds and to understanding the part you play in each. Here is a summary of what we covered in this chapter:

- Even though codependency is sometimes referred to as relationship addiction and is often thought of in connection with romance, this unhealthy and often one-sided attachment can form in any relationship.

- When creating boundaries, the five key areas to focus on are our personal boundaries, sexual boundaries, financial boundaries, emotional boundaries, and time boundaries.

- As you begin enforcing new boundaries, be prepared for turbulence in your relationships initially. After all, no one likes change, and boundaries can feel like rejection or abandonment to some.

- When issues arise in your relationships, the ego, in its attempt to keep you safe, will try to convince you that it is all the fault of the other person or people involved. The truth is, it always takes two to tango, and if your relationships are strained, on some level you are contributing to that strain.

- Our closest connections with others can serve as a valuable tool for self-discovery.

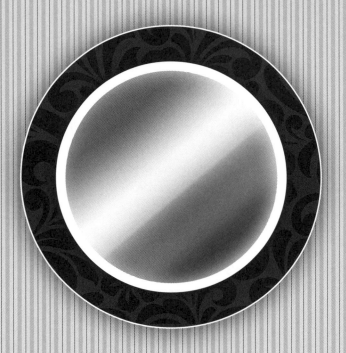

JOURNAL
PAGES

Identify a person with whom you have a strained relationship. Write both your names in the middle of the circle below. Next, fill in the circle with positive words and phrases that either describe that person or the energy you wish to call in to your relationship with them. For example, you may say things like "improved communication," "love," "generosity," "kindness," "compassion," or "healing." Allow intuition to be your guide. If resistance shows up, breathe in the energy of love. When you have filled in your circle, write the words "It is done. Thank you, thank you, thank you," all the way around the outside of the circle.

When you are in strife with those in your life, you may focus on the other person and neglect to look at your own contributing actions. Take a look at how you may be creating issues in your relationships and write about it here.

How can you consciously shift your mindset to focus on more positive aspects of your troubled relationships? How can you be more accountable for the issues in your relationships to which you may be contributing?

_____

_____

_____

_____

_____

_____

_____

_____

_____

_____

_____

_____

_____

_____

_____

_____

The relationship you have with yourself sets the tone for every other relationship in your life. When you have a healthy love of self, you naturally create healthy boundaries that are aligned with your self-worth. Write a love letter to yourself. If you feel stumped, think about your biggest insecurities or what you're the hardest on yourself about, then write loving and reassuring messages around those things. When you are finished, go to the mirror and read your love letter back to yourself while making eye contact. Read your letter to yourself daily.

How did resistance show up while writing and then reading your letter to yourself? What other actions can you take to improve the quality of the relationship you have with yourself?

Many people hold a limiting belief that it's conceited to praise, honor, and adore themselves. How comfortable are you with thinking and saying positive things about yourself? How comfortable are you with receiving compliments from others? Was there a person in your past who made you feel as if you weren't worthy of love? If so, how did that impact your current view of yourself?

Forgiveness can be a difficult lesson. The ego holds grudges, creating resistance to forgiveness. Forgiving does not mean you condone wrongdoing. It just means choosing to set yourself free of anger. This requires practice. Think of someone you have a grudge against. Once you have brought the person and the circumstance to mind, work through this exercise.

_____ *[name of the person]*,

I wish you _____ *[set a positive*

intention like health, wealth, love, happiness, etc.].

Repeat this four more times with a new positive intention each time:

_____

_____

_____

_____

When you finish, read what you wrote aloud while choosing to genuinely feel the energy of the well-wishes. Do this five times. Then, take a deep breath and release any resistance that showed up during this exercise.

What did you find most difficult about the forgiveness exercise? How did your ego respond to sending good intentions to someone who offended or harmed you in some way? What big emotions showed up for you during this exercise? How did you feel after completing it?

Embrace Your Shadow for Lasting Self-Love

The real invitation in the shadow work journey is one of self-love, self-acceptance, and self-compassion. As you embrace these key concepts, every other relationship in your life is improved as a result.

We are inundated with societal pressure to look a certain way as unrealistic lifestyles are glamorized, leaving so many feeling as if they have somehow fallen short or missed the mark. In this chapter, however, you will focus on building the most substantial and most loving relationship with yourself by learning to fully love and accept all aspects of yourself, especially your shadow.

By shedding the limiting beliefs created around the subliminal messages that surround us all, you can learn not only to love yourself entirely but also to truly connect to and understand yourself in ways you never have before. Each time we shed an outdated version of ourselves, we are asked to become reacquainted with the new version. This process, like most, is never-ending; awareness is simply deepened.

Self-Awareness Leads to Clarity

As part of my intake process, I send each client with whom I work a questionnaire to complete before their first session. Many questions are used to gauge how much clarity a client has around their desires, goals, and motivations. It's not uncommon for people to respond with statements like "I don't know," "That's a good question," or "I'm not sure." While the question may be about nailing down their short- and long-term goals, understanding their passions and desires sometimes leads clients to these answers. After all, how can you know what goals you have if you don't even know what you enjoy doing?

Consider the case of Jamie, for example. Jamie was one of the more challenging clients I've worked with in this regard. For the first three sessions, she answered almost every question with uncertainty.

I quickly realized that Jamie had to rediscover herself. In time, she revealed that after giving birth to her sons, she felt as if she had lost herself in the titles of mother and wife and no longer knew who she was outside of them. I created a plan for her that slowly led her to self-discovery, which helped her gain clarity in the previously uncertain areas we had discussed. Finally, we were able to get her on track to accomplishing her newly discovered goals of making and selling jewelry in her spare time.

EXPLORING WHAT LIGHTS YOU UP AND BRINGS YOU JOY

The road to self-discovery is a never-ending and winding one. As new experiences are presented and we are transformed through growth, we are called to this discovery of self, time and time again.

Fill in the blanks to help you gain insight into what excites you and lights you up.

Time flies when I am

The activities I find most enjoyable are

I love spending my free time

If I could make a living doing whatever I wanted, I would choose

I feel most carefree when I am

I wish I had more time to

I want to learn more about

I have a burning in my belly to accomplish

I find the following topics interesting:

I feel light and uplifted when I spend time with

MORE OF WHAT YOU ENJOY

What did you discover about yourself, your passions, and your desires from the fill-in-the-blank exercise? What excuses or limiting beliefs come to mind that prevent you from doing more of what you enjoy?

FOLLOW YOUR BLISS

When we do more of what lights our soul up and brings us joy, we attract more positive experiences and opportunities. For this practice, apply what you have discovered here and commit to carving out more time for doing what you deeply enjoy.

How can you make more space in your life to do more of these things, and what would those things be? Get specific on what these activities look like and when you will make the time in your life for them. Is it taking a class to learn more about a topic of interest, spending more time with a particularly uplifting person, planning more travel, or maybe creating more time for hobbies?

Make time each day to do more of what brings you joy with intentionality. Record your experience in a journal for reference later. You never know where it will lead. Five years ago, choosing to walk every morning while listening to an inspirational podcast led me to writing three books and running my own business, and I never saw that coming. Life has a way of unfolding in the most magical ways when we slip into the present moment and embrace it with joyfulness.

What does your ideal life, in which there are no limitations, look and feel like? What do you truly and deeply desire once all restraints are removed?

GETTING CLEAR ON YOUR GOALS

Shadow work is all about illuminating the unknown. Most people probably don't think of goal-setting as part of shadow work. However, understanding and knowing yourself well enough to know what goals are important to you is a substantial piece of the puzzle.

Use this chart to define your immediate, short-term, and long-term goals.

Immediate Goals: Goals you can work toward and achieve reasonably quickly and easily

Examples: *Take a weekend trip or visit a lonely family member*

Goal 1	
Goal 2	
Goal 3	

Short-Term Goals: Goals that will take you one to two years to achieve
Examples: *Saving for a large expense or writing a book*

Long-Term Goals*: Goals that are five or more years down the road
Examples: *Owning your dream home, traveling the world, or running your own business*

	Short-Term	Long-Term
Goal 1		
Goal 2		
Goal 3		

*Don't allow the ego to convince you that some goals are "too big." Reference the journal prompt before this exercise and use that as your guide for creating these long-term goals.

I clear away anything and everything that stands in the way of me experiencing my highest expression of joy.

(You may work with this affirmation on a deeper level by clearly identifying what blocks you from joyfulness.)

MAKING YOUR DREAMS COME TRUE

Now that you have set clear-cut goals, it's time to get started on bringing these into reality. Accomplishing anything we desire happens in a series of small, manageable steps, each bringing us that much closer to where we want to be. The only difference between those who succeed and those who do not is their willingness to stay on the path and be patient with the process.

Say that an individual has a goal to become a motivational speaker and stand on a stage in front of thousands of people. Let's also say that tomorrow, they wake up, and this dream has magically become their new reality. Now it's time for them to step out onto that stage, but they skipped all the steps that led them to this point, so they are completely unprepared and not yet qualified to hold this role. Could you imagine how terrifying that would be? Something that is supposed to be their dream come true may instead feel like a nightmare. We need the processes, the failures we learn from, and the education we gain on our way to achieving our big goals.

This practice is about taking small actionable but achievable steps toward your desires. Choose one goal from each category—immediate, short-term, and long-term—and then decide on one actionable step you can take for each. An individual who wants to be a well-known motivational speaker may start a blog or take a speechwriting class. Make sure you set a time limit on this (e.g., "I will enroll in a speechwriting class by the end of the week" or "I will have a platform for my blog by the end of this month").

Work through your list and continue creating new goals as you have more experiences through this process.

EMBRACING YOUR SHADOW ASPECTS WITH LOVE

It's essential to accept your imperfections without allowing the fact that you have them to lead you to emotions like guilt, shame, or feeling less than. We all fall short of perfection, and there is no shame in acknowledging where improvement is needed.

In this exercise, you will identify and confront your shortcomings and then practice extending love and compassion to yourself for each. The more comfortable you are engaging your shadow with love and acceptance, the more quickly you can identify areas of concern and make adjustments that feel in line with your core values.

First identify one of your shortcomings. Underneath each identifying statement you create, you will write an affirming statement. Each affirming statement should address the perceived shortcoming and then end with "but I still fully love, honor, and accept myself."

Example:

Shortcoming: I am sometimes dishonest with my partner to keep the peace.

Affirming Statement: I am a work in progress and don't always act in ways that are aligned with my core values because of my fear of confrontation, but I still fully love, honor, and accept myself.

Shortcoming: _____

Affirming Statement: _____

Shortcoming: _____

Affirming Statement: _____

Shortcoming: _____

Affirming Statement: _____

Shortcoming: _____

Affirming Statement: _____

ADJUSTING YOUR BEHAVIOR

What is the root cause of some of the shortcomings you identified in the exercise? Reflect on how you can adjust your behavior to improve in these areas.

MIRROR WORK PRACTICE

Mirror work is performed when we connect with ourselves using a mirror as a tool. For this practice, you will take time each day for at least twenty-one days to speak loving words to yourself while making eye contact in the mirror. This is a practice that can fit easily into your morning routine while you are dressing for the day.

Mirror work can be highly uncomfortable, and you may even feel silly and worry about what others may think if they hear you. I encourage you to push past these fears and discomforts and commit to the practice. I've listed a few phrases you can use to start with, but customize your statements based on what you need to hear.

Example statements:

- I love you.

- You are so beautiful inside and out.

- I am so proud of you.

- You are doing great!

- You are so worthy.

- You are perfectly imperfect, and that's okay!

- You matter.

What are some of the more profound truths you discovered about yourself through this shadow work journey? How has this awareness changed your perception of yourself and your experiences?

_____

_____

_____

_____

_____

_____

_____

_____

_____

*I can achieve anything I set my mind to if
I am dedicated and consistent.*

FINAL REFLECTIONS

This final exercise will bring awareness to how you have grown through this process, highlight your wins, and help you reflect on the positive shifts that have transpired because of your hard work, dedication, and commitment to your personal growth and transformation.

In what ways has your mindset improved from the shadow work you have done?

What wins have you experienced because of the inner work you have done?

How have your relationships improved?

What were some "aha!" moments you experienced while working through the workbook?

How has this work changed the way you think and feel about yourself?

How have your fears worked to keep you small, and what steps have you taken, or will take, to confront these fears?

CELEBRATING YOURSELF

Even though this is a fun practice, celebrating ourselves can feel uncomfortable. Being in the spotlight may make some feel as if they are being conceited or attention-seeking, but nothing could be further from the truth. Being able to celebrate your wins comfortably is a sign of healthy confidence.

If you have made it to this final exercise, working through the activities and practices diligently, you should be beaming with pride. This is worth celebrating, and that is precisely what you will be asked to do in this last assignment.

Plan something fun for yourself to commemorate your journey through the shadows. It could be treating yourself to a nice dinner out with your partner or close friends, or taking a relaxing weekend trip. You may buy yourself your favorite flowers or finally book that spa day you have been dreaming about. This will look different for everyone. Be intentional with what you choose, and know you are so worth it!

Key Takeaways

This final chapter was focused on helping you not only find a deeper under-standing of yourself but also accept all aspects of yourself, including your shadow. Here are the key points to keep in mind:

- The road to self-discovery is a never-ending and winding one. As new experiences are presented and we are transformed through growth, we are called to this discovery of self, time and time again.

- When we do more of what lights our soul up and brings us joy, we attract more positive experiences and opportunities.

- Most people may not think of goal-setting as part of shadow work. However, understanding and knowing yourself well enough to know what goals are important to you is a substantial piece of the puzzle.

- It's essential to accept your imperfections without allowing them to lead you to emotions like guilt, shame, or feeling less than.

- Being able to celebrate your wins comfortably is a sign of healthy confidence.

JOURNAL
PAGES

Love is an energy that you can choose to embody, and it will support you in accepting all aspects of yourself. Most shadow work is focused on how to improve the negative aspects of yourself that hide in the shadows, but I want to flip the script and invite some balance by bringing your attention to what you love about your life. List anything in your current experience that connects you to love. It could be people, places, pets, songs, activities, or anything else. Revisit this page anytime you need a boost of love's healing energy.

1. _____

2. _____

3. _____

4. _____

5. _____

6. _____

7. _____

8. _____

9. _____

10. _____

Looking at your list, how often do you engage in activities, situations, or with people that activate the energy of love? How can you carve out more time to devote to these things, and how would that look? How might your life change if you consciously focused daily on being an embodiment of love?

Think about certain behaviors in others about which you have harsh or judgmental views. How might you approach this person, their behaviors, or the situation with more compassion and love? Your ego will try to resist this approach, so stay vigilant of this tendency and return to a space of love if you notice such resistance.

The thirty-second hug is also known as the oxytocin hug because of the hormone released during extended periods of physical touch. The release of oxytocin eases anxiety and counteracts stress hormones. It also regulates the nervous system, promoting physical and emotional health.

Start by giving yourself thirty-second hugs periodically throughout the day. Aim for about three times a day: morning, afternoon, and evening. If you have a hard time remembering, try setting a reminder on your phone.

You can also induce the release of oxytocin by practicing extending long hugs to your partner, children, best friend, or family members.

☐ **Before the hug:** Take a deep breath and notice how you feel before the thirty-second hug. In the first box below, note what you feel in your body or your energy. For example, do you feel tightness in your chest, anxious, heaviness somewhere in your body, and so on?

☐ **After the hug:** Take another deep breath once you have finished and tune in to your body, mind, and spirit once again. Note the shift in the second box below.

How I feel before

How I feel after

When you identify with certain aspects of the shadow, you may behave out of alignment with your core values. Awareness of your tendencies allows you the opportunity to align with your higher self and stay true to your core values. Use the following checklist to identify ways you find yourself acting outside of your integral belief system.

☐ Yelling

☐ Name-calling

☐ Gossiping

☐ Judging and comparing

☐ Dishonesty

☐ Competitiveness

☐ Stubbornness

☐ Holding grudges

☐ Seeking outside validation

☐ Self-sabotage

☐ Envy

☐ Greed

☐ Selfishness

☐ People-pleasing

☐ Reactiveness

☐ Impatience

☐ Spitefulness

How have your core values changed over time? What values and ideas did the adults in your life instill in you as a child? Have these changed in adulthood?

_____

_____

_____

_____

_____

_____

_____

_____

What values are most important to you in the following areas:

Family life: _____

Romantic relationships: _____

Work: _____

Friendships: _____

Relationship with self: _____

WRITING A NEW STORY

It is often the stories birthed from our childhood experiences that keep us stuck in our toxic cycles and patterns. Writing a new narrative can move us to a healthier space and ultimately reshape our current experience. This exercise has two parts. First, you must identify your old stories, and then you must create something new. For example, a person who grew up with a mother who often criticized them and placed unrealistic expectations on them may have grown into an adult with people-pleasing tendencies. Because of this, they created a story that says that to be worthy of love and acceptance, they must please others. A new, more helpful story might be that they are worthy of love, affection, validation, and appreciation with no strings attached. Use this exercise to guide you through rewriting one of your own stories.

Identify a long-held narrative and use the space to write about it.

A Final Word

Congratulations! I am so incredibly proud of you, and hopefully you are, too. This is not work for the faint of heart, and we went deep with several shadow work topics.

Hopefully, you have learned a lot about yourself, your experiences, and the world around you through your shadow work journey. I want to express my deep gratitude to you for sticking with it and committing to your personal growth.

Now it's time to enjoy the fruits of your labor and all your hard work. While much growth does happen through difficult, uncomfortable, and even painful experiences, growth is also offered to us through joyfulness. Lean in with the understanding that you can grow through love and grace.

Thank you so much for allowing me to be a part of your journey; this is something I never take for granted. It is my most profound honor and calling to guide others through this work, so thank you for giving me the space to fulfill my purpose, one word at a time. I hope that I have served this calling well.

So much love to you all.

—Kelly

Resources

Carl Jung: Knowledge in a Nutshell, by Gary Bobroff
> This is an easy-to-understand introduction to Carl Jung's life and the beliefs he formed and shared centered around the subconscious mind.

Co-Dependents Anonymous, coda.org
> A twelve-step community program to help support people who struggle to make healthy relationships.

How to Do the Work: Recognize Your Patterns, Heal from Your Past, and Create Your Self, by Dr. Nicole LePera
> Learn how to recognize limiting belief patterns and confront conditioned thinking to reconnect with your true self.

It Didn't Start with You: How Inherited Family Trauma Shapes Who We Are and How to End the Cycle, by Mark Wolynn
> This book serves as an exploration of the connection between generational wounds and anxiety, depression, chronic pain, and other mental and physical disorders.

Kelly Bramblett's *High Vibe* **(podcast, available on all major streaming platforms)**
> In my *High Vibe* podcast, I and my many guest speakers guide you through a plethora of shadow work topics.

Rewired (TV show), hosted by Dr. Joe Dispenza
> Explore your subconscious mind and learn how to rewire your brain so you can form healthy habits, confront your shadow, and heal your trauma.

SelfHealers Soundboard with Dr. Nicole LePera and Jenna Weakland (podcast)
> In this podcast, you'll learn how to recognize and confront your patterns, heal your past painful experiences, and develop a deeper understanding of self.

Your Inner Child: A Guided Journal to Heal Your Past and Recover Your Joy, by Kelly Bramblett
> In this book I provide writing prompts and thoughtful practices to help you heal your inner child and embrace a more fulfilling future.

REFERENCES

Centers for Disease Control and Prevention. "Heart Disease and Mental Health Disorders." Last modified May 6, 2020. cdc.gov/heartdisease/mentalhealth.htm.

Centers for Disease Control and Prevention. "What Is Epigenetics?" Last modified August 3, 2020. cdc.gov/genomics/disease/epigenetics.htm.

Index

trust, 45

truth, confronting uncomfortable, 30–32

U

unconscious mind, 6, 9, 79

uniqueness, embracing, 38–40

V

values, core, 182–183

vulnerability, 16, 27, 41, 44–45, 51

W

walls, self-constructed, 28, 41

weird, meaning of, 38

well-being, 9

wounds, 17–18, 107

  healing, 14

ABOUT THE AUTHOR

Kelly Bramblett is a fully certified general life coach, trauma care specialist, law of attraction practitioner, emotional freedom technique (EFT) practitioner, and level III Usui Reiki Master teacher who specializes in trauma recovery and mind-set coaching. Kelly also writes a weekly spirituality-based blog and is the host of Kelly Bramblett's *High Vibe* podcast, which can be heard on all major streaming platforms.

Kelly's mission is to spread a message of hope and inspire others to heal the collective by first healing themselves.

Her first book, *Alchemy of the Phoenix: From the Ashes of Trauma to the Light of Love*, was written to offer support for trauma survivors worldwide.